Marion Debruyne &
Katleen De Stobbeleir

Making your way

The (wobbly) road to success and happiness in life and work

Lannoo

www.lannoo.com

Second print run, 2020

Register on our website to receive a regular newsletter with information about new books and interesting exclusive offers.

COVER: Studio Lannoo (Nele Reyniers)
COVER PICTURE: Björn Comhaire
LAYOUT: Studio Lannoo (Nele Reyniers)

D/2020/45/573 – ISBN 978 94 014 7276 0 – NUR 770/801

CONTENTS

We are
all works in
progress.

Preface - Making it, your way

Be the hero(ine) of your own life.

Nora Ephron

A real gentleman does not discuss the women he's broken up with, the taxes he pays, or what he does to stay healthy. That's what Haruki Murakami, one of our favorite novelists, wrote in his inspiring memoirs. He, of course, made up this saying. But if there really were such a saying, it would probably also say that a real gentleman should keep quiet about what he does to be successful in life.

We're not gentlemen. So we shouldn't be worrying about this in the first place. But we admit that, just as Haruki Murakami felt hesitant about writing his own memoirs, we felt some hesitation about writing this book ... a book about career success and living a purposeful life. After all, who are we to tell you what to do? The last thing we wanted to do is to write a recipe book. The type of book that is full of advice that says: 'Ok, everybody – read this and you'll be successful. Follow our recipes and, whoosh, all of your troubles will go away.'

We want to encourage people to set themselves free from such myths and to pursue their dreams with confidence and optimism.

Yet we do need to talk about it. About what it takes to thrive in today's world. That mission is close to our hearts. Because of our work, as a business school dean (Marion) and leadership expert and personal coach (Katleen), we touch the lives of so many students and young professionals. It is our professional duty to think about the messages we want to convey to them. We wrote this book for them. We often meet people who have amazing potential but who don't realize that potential because of some limiting beliefs about what a career and happiness should look like. We want to encourage people to set themselves free from such myths and to pursue their dreams with confidence and optimism.

In every chapter of this book, we tackle one of those myths that we often encounter. We hope you find inspiration in each of the 15 chapters we have written, whether you are a young student embarking on your career, or a seasoned leader looking for new insights. With this book we hope to stimulate you to **live** your dream and pursue your goals. That requires living with intention, which is the focus of our first five chapters. Call us naïve, but we believe that dreams can come true. Yet not necessarily like in fairy tales. To live your dream, you need to pursue it, and be willing to stumble and **learn** every day. And even though we work at a business school, we're not just talking about the learning you do in the classroom. It's about challenging yourself in different areas of life. More about that in chapters 6-10. After all, everyone has potential to make it. All it takes is a little bit of guts to **take the leap**. In chapters 11-15 we discuss how that feels, and the ripple effect that you can set in motion. After all: no guts, no glory. By pure coincidence, you may recognize Vlerick Business School's Live-Learn-Leap credo.

The journey to happiness in both work and life is most often a messy one. And that's ok. We are all works in progress.

In an effort to gain insight into our personal experiences and the stories we encounter, we dove into the research. That helped us to discover that personal stories contain universal truths. You will find these under the heading "What we know for sure". (A shameless rip-off of how Oprah Winfrey describes her personal life lessons.) As academics, in science we trust, so we're only sure when we find the research to back up our claims.

This book does contain a certain amount of what might be called life lessons: both our own life lessons (and we're hopefully only halfway through our own lives!), and also the life lessons of the people we were fortunate enough to meet and talk to. They are personal lessons, and that's also what this book is to us —personal. As professionals, mothers, wives, friends — juggling many roles — there is one thing we really know for sure: every picture-perfect moment hides a less glamorous reality. As Indra Nooyi's mom told her when she became global president of PepsiCo: 'Leave the crown in the garage'. So, as ambitious as the title of this book may be, its subtitle reveals the other side of the coin: that the journey to happiness in both work and life is most often a wobbly one. And that's ok. We are all works in progress.

So we have left our crowns in the garage, in an effort to keep it real and reveal the mistakes, the doubts, and the slip-ups that are part of even the most seamlessly upward career. Many of the lessons we present in this book are lessons that we also had to learn, sometimes the hard way. The things we would like to tell our younger selves. The things we wish we had known.

We present the things we would like to tell our younger selves. The things we wish we had known.

We've written honestly about what we think and feel and we have tried to stay true to our own styles. And this book is really the product of two very different styles ... brought together in the same way that a jazz combo plays together. Without talking, following each other's leads, and adding to each other's written words on the page.

"Take it from us" is the message you will find at the end of each chapter. However, the most important take-away is this one: Don't follow our recipes too closely ... add your own grain of salt (or pepper or whatever spice you fancy)! Everybody's story is unique. There is no recipe book for life. So off you go, carve your own path, and make your own decisions. Making it, your unique way.

Do you even
dare to say
out loud
what it is
you are
dreaming of?

1 Feel the fire in the belly

The myth: you can be anything you want to be

It always seems impossible until it's done.

Nelson Mandela

'Shoot for the moon. Even if you miss, you'll still be among the stars.' That's how the saying goes. So are you shooting for the moon? Or are you keeping yourself to more modest goals? Do you even dare to say out loud what it is you are dreaming of? It takes guts to do so. Take Felix van de Maele, co-founder and CEO of Collibra. Felix started the company while he was still a student, together with 3 other friends. At the time, the company was a pioneer in data governance. Less than a decade later, the start-up became a unicorn: a company less than 10 years old, but nevertheless valued at more than a billion dollars. This was already a formidable accomplishment. But when asked about how he felt about realizing that milestone, Felix only said: 'I'm not really thinking about it. I'm now already thinking more about how we will get to 5 billion in value.'

Is this going to be one of those books that tells you how to get to that 5 billion? Far from it. Because that may not be your goal at all. Or you may have no clue what your goal is yet. And that's ok. You'll discover it along the way. Very few people have dreams and goals as explicit as Felix's. Yours may be much less clear. But no matter how big or small, explicit or vague your dreams are, none of them will come true without chasing them.

So, yes, this is going to be one of those books. About the wobbly road to happiness and success, whatever your definition of happiness and success is. We'll share with you a few things we have discovered along the way. Through the people we were fortunate to meet. Through the research that we, as academics, can't help but dive into in the search for wisdom. And the many times we learned a lesson ourselves the hard way. Are you coming with us on the journey? Then read on!

The power of dreams

Dreaming big propels you forward.

'What do you want to be when you grow up?' It's a simple question that virtually every child on the planet can answer in a snap. For many years, Marion wanted to become a ballerina, while Katleen dreamed of being a cook or a fiction writer. Look at how that turned out. Very few of us actually go on and realize our childhood dreams. Not even someone like Richard Branson from Virgin, who dreamed of being a poet. Despite all those unmaterialized childhood dreams, growing up doesn't mean that we should stop dreaming altogether. In fact, if you think about it, dreams are the source of most human progress.

President John F. Kennedy (who actually did want to become a president when he grew up) dreamed of putting a (wo)man on the moon ... and he mobilized an entire nation to make it happen. It was literally a moonshot project. Pledging to achieve something as big as going to the moon is probably as crazy as buying a lottery ticket against all the odds. So why did a previously unthinkable dream inspire and generate so much human effort that they actually made it happen? For the same reason that people buy that lottery ticket. It gave them an opportunity to dream. And in dreams, we invest.

Dreaming big propels you forward. Even when your dream, or the way that you could realize it, isn't clear-cut. That's because small dreams lead to small thinking, whereas big dreams lead to big thinking. That's the logic behind X, the innovation lab from Alphabet (the mother company of Google), which is literally called the Moonshot Factory. X embodies a radical way of thinking by taking crazy ideas seriously. In order to be considered a moonshot, an idea must fulfill three criteria: it must address a significant global problem, involve inventing breakthrough technology, and result in a radical outcome—at least "10X" better than what exists today. The 10 actually means 10 times better. That's because making something 10 times better leads to totally different thinking than making something 10% better. Let's say you wanted to create a car that has 10% less CO_2 emissions. Then you would probably work on making the car incrementally better by increasing its fuel efficiency. But let's say you wanted to make a car that was 10 times better than that. That would force you to adopt a radically different approach and a complete rethink about the way the car works. Like Elon Musk has done by creating Tesla, the entirely electronic vehicle.

During our lives we've already witnessed quite a few moonshot businesses, products, and projects that literally changed the world. Tim Berners-Lee did it when he created the internet. Apple's iPhone was definitely a moonshot project. And, more recently, you have probably also been staring into the night sky to watch the "Starlink train" from SpaceX fly by.

When we witness such human progress, we just feel that anything is possible. Yet, when it comes to ourselves, we see limits everywhere.

So why wouldn't you shoot for the moon? What is your moonshot project? Naïve, you say? Maybe. But perhaps we should all be a bit more naïve. Think of Boyan Slat, a Dutch inventor and entrepreneur who, at the age of 18, founded The Ocean Cleanup, a project focused on getting rid of all of the plastic in our oceans. The project started when Boyan went diving, but saw more plastic than actual fish. He started a mission to clean up all of the earth's oceans from the plastic soup that littered them. The Ocean Cleanup gathered millions of euros from crowdfunding and donations, which have been invested in developing a giant floating interceptor to "catch" all of the waste that floats on our waters. Boyan's moonshot dream spurred a quest of discovery and technological progress, from the early prototype to the current models that are tested in the waters around Jamaica and Malaysia.

What we know for sure: characteristics of successful moonshot projects

Moonshots might sound like long shots, but they aren't. In an inspiring article, Sue Ashford, who recently received a lifetime achievement award for her own moonshot contributions to management science, uses the 1991 movie *Thelma and Louise* as a metaphor to disentangle the characteristics of successful moonshot projects. *Thelma and Louise* is an American road movie about two female buddies who go on a road trip to get a break from their dull lives. During a stop at a roadhouse bar, Thelma gets sexually harassed. Louise murders the harasser in a flare of blind rage. They decide to go on the run, and the movie shows a terrifying escape from being hunted by the police before coming to a dramatic end with the two ladies taking their own lives by driving their car into the Grand Canyon. It is considered to be an epic movie that has globally changed the conversation about gender. Sue Ashford describes some of the ingredients that made the movie so impactful and that are applicable to any successful moonshot project. First, the idea on which the movie was based was important. It was a simple and communicable idea: two women that go on a crime spree. It's as simple as that. And this goes for moonshot projects as well. The Ocean Cleanup is about removing plastic from the oceans. And the Starlink project aims to provide everyone with internet access. Second, the movie was timely. Even though a female road buddy movie hadn't been made before, it fit in very well with a growing movement in the US that stood up for women's rights. Likewise, moonshot projects fit the "zeitgeist". An app like "Too Good To Go", which connects consumers with unsold food from a variety of shops and restaurants, would probably not be as successful if there wasn't a zeitgeist that emphasizes sustainability. The movie was personally relevant to the screenwriter, Callie Khouri, who had been assaulted twice herself. It always helps to be personally involved in whatever moonshot project you pursue. Think of Martine Rothblatt, who was on the verge of retirement after creating satellite radio with a startup that went on to become Sirius XM.

But her daughter's rare lung disease inspired her to start United Therapeutics and develop an oral medication that changed the lives of thousands of patients. This very personal project made her the highest-paid female executive in the US in 2013. It also made her the nation's highest-paid transgendered person.

Of course, in a moonshot project, it's not just the idea that matters. So does the process. Often you'll hear coaches say "Trust the process". Advice like this may sound like a lot of empty words to you, but when you think of it, it's actually phenomenal advice. When you aim for the moon, there will be plenty of moments where you don't trust yourself. And you don't need to. If you don't trust yourself, just trust the process. Stick to a well-grounded methodology, a long-term plan even in the face of short term outcomes and stick to it with determination. Dare to down-value short-term wins in favor of the long term. After all, moonshot projects require intense work, an eye for detail, and overcoming obstacles with the support of others. Of course, a moonshot project wouldn't be a moonshot project if there wasn't a little controversy and a little sex appeal. *Thelma and Louise* was controversial and generated quite a number of reactions. And we don't need to beat around the bush about it: Brad Pitt helped with the sex appeal.

Perhaps the most important lesson came from the movie's tagline: "You get what you settle for". In other words, if you aim low, you'll also end low. Don't think you'll do your important work later. Dare to aim high right from the start.

Ashford, S. J. (2013). Having Scholarly Impact: The Art of Hitting Academic Home Runs. *Academy of Management Learning & Education*, 12(4), 623–633.

Great expectations

Shooting for the moon is surprisingly hard. It's scary. To say it out loud that you aim to make it big. You may fall flat on your face. And the thought of those embarrassing comments, such as "Told you so". Is your dream really worth all of that? With great expectations comes the chance of great disappointment. What we know for sure is that if you don't think you'll succeed, then you won't give it your best shot. And an entire series of half-hearted shots will undermine your chances of ever pulling it off. Yes, your ego might get bruised in the process, but Ross Edgley was right: you should be naïve enough to start, but stubborn enough to finish. (He himself was naïve enough to start a swim all around Great Britain, and apparently stubborn enough to finish it. He swam for an entire 157 days without setting a foot on land in order to swim around the entire 3,200 km coastline).

Interestingly, most of us have an even bigger fear than the fear of failure. We dread success and the price we'll pay to achieve it.

Interestingly, most of us have an even bigger fear than the fear of failure. We dread success and the price we'll pay to achieve it. We avoid success because we feel we don't deserve it or because we don't like the feeling of defeating others. Success is frightening because it creates expectations, especially the expectation that the success will need to continue. And the bigger your role, the more that people depend on you and care what you do and say.

Don't underestimate the toll of success. Accomplishments have a tendency to weigh on you ... or as Sigmund Freud would say: you can become "wrecked by success". Think of the many stories about athletes and artists who were propelled from relative anonymity into a public life of glamour, and were not ready for that type of success and ended up sabotaging themselves. But does it really have to be that way?

What we know for sure: why we dread success

We can learn a lot about the fear of success from golden oldie studies on athletic performance. One of these studies, from 1968 (apparently the sixties were productive for moonshot thinking!), explored why athletes worried about aiming high. The study revealed that athletes had five key concerns that held them back from giving it their all. First, many of them worried about the social and emotional isolation that would come with the long road to success ... after all, it can get pretty lonely at the top. And what if you put in a lot of "lonely" hard work and you don't even reach the top? Athletes also expressed guilt about asserting themselves in an aggressive or competitive manner. This concern was particularly strong among women, who felt that it was inappropriate for them to be competitive. Even though this study was done in the sixties, research shows that women in business today often still feel this way. The study also revealed that many athletes worried that their true potential would be revealed (read: that their true limits would be exposed). Others felt concerned about surpassing someone they admired and about being resented by the person they admired the most. The most common source of fear of success, however, was the fear of having to deal with the constant pressure of maintaining success and living up to the expectations of others. It just felt safer to stay in the shadows. Do any of these reasons sound familiar to you? What can you do about it? Admitting to yourself that you are self-sabotaging by being afraid of success is half the battle. And the other half is probably to remember that, in order to really be able to do moonshot thinking, you need to not only embrace your strengths, but also come to terms with your weaknesses. And the two are very related. Being a high achiever can be rewarding, but the behaviors that help you to succeed can also get in your way. If you take for granted the things that make you stand out from the crowd, you'll never shine. But if you don't own the weaknesses that come with those talents, this will slow you down. So moonshot thinking requires self-awareness and the ability to accept yourself. And some hard work too.

Ogilivie, B. C. (1968). The Unconscious Fear of Success. *Quest,* 10, 35-39.

Fire in the belly

Edison said: 'Vision without execution is just hallucination.' Simply wanting something is not enough. The way to achieve something big is to start small—the same way that you would build a muscle in the gym. And we know how that works; you start small (unless you like to overstretch yourself) and you start to train that muscle consistently ... and patiently! And that's where we often give up on our dream: because we aren't pursuing it consistently and with patience. Bill Gates put it well: 'Most people overestimate what they can do in one year and underestimate what they can do in ten years.' So having a dream isn't enough, you also need "follow-through". And that is hard work. Success really is only 1% inspiration and 99% perspiration. Just having a good idea or raw talent simply doesn't cut it. You need enough fire in the belly to keep going.

And that fire or determination isn't genetic, it's something that you constantly need to feed. All you need is a little spark, but it's up to you to keep on feeding that spark so that it becomes a raging fire. And that's part of the process of moonshot thinking: keeping yourself motivated to keep going.

Mette Lykke, CEO of Too Good To Go, calls this "patient impatience": 'Every day you have to push yourself and you have to do that for quite a while. We need the sense of urgency in building our company because speed is really important. We want to inspire 250 million people to change their behavior around food waste and we want to save 1 billion meals. It matters if a new account is closed on Friday instead of Monday. The faster we grow, the more meals are saved from being wasted. Then the patience part is about understanding that we have to do this many days in a row to see the impact. We don't move mountains in twenty-four hours, so we need patience. I initially constantly had this feeling that I was climbing a mountain but I could see the flag at the top. Yet once you get to the top you can actually already see a bigger mountain behind it. And you go again.'

It's up to you to keep on feeding that spark so that it becomes a raging fire.

One of the core ideas at Google's X division is "Monkey First". What this means is the following: 'If you were asked to teach a monkey to stand on a pedestal and recite Shakespeare, you should resist starting with the simplest task (building the pedestal) and start with the hardest (teaching a monkey to speak).'

Now, think of yourself as the monkey. Just kidding. Or maybe not. Because we all have "those days", the days where we would rather do the easy stuff than the hard stuff. The days that distract us from our bigger goals. We get distracted by side projects. Or we just postpone our big dream, because "the time is just not right". Psychologists would call this procrastination. We often see procrastination as a form of laziness or poor time management. But is that really true? Someone who gets distracted by firefighting or by helping others can hardly be called lazy. Then why do we get distracted? As it turns out, it's because big dreams come with big emotions. Developing that start-up, developing a solution for climate change, or even achieving a goal such as eating healthily can just feel too difficult, too tedious, or ... too scary. Let's face it: no one dreams of getting up at 5.30 am to go running because their big dream is to do a marathon. That's just difficult. Our emotions around pursuing big dreams mean that we invest disproportional amounts of time on things that we don't really care about. Let's face it, the time you spend on binge-watching the latest Netflix series won't help you go after what you really want.

So how do you begin working toward that dream? Just do it.

So how do you begin working toward that dream? Just do it! Peter Diamandis, co-founder of Singularity University, put it like this: 'Lots of people dream big and talk about big bold ideas but never do anything. I judge people by what they've done. The ratio of something to nothing is infinite. So just do something.'

The reality of every moonshot challenge is that it consists of lots and lots of small steps. So just start walking. Some self-talk might help (yes, finally a book that gives you an excuse to talk to yourself). And be smart on those self-rewards. Treat yourself to that coffee or Netflix episode after you have taken a step toward that bigger goal, rather than pouring yourself a cup of courage before getting started.

And you know what, sometimes you just need to trick yourself. For example, if you really want to go for that marathon, why not put on your sports gear before you go to bed to make sure you do not keep pushing the snooze button when your alarm goes off. Or if you really want to write that book, make sure that when you open your laptop, the first thing you see is a half-finished sentence from your next chapter. It's just like in the gym: if you're waiting for 2 undisturbed weeks to start exercising, you won't build any muscles. And if you want to write a business plan, it's probably an illusion to wait until you have a full month to work on it. Get yourself started by committing to 15 minutes every day ... but do accept that sometimes you'll just have some of "those" days.

If you really want to go for that marathon, why not put on your sports gear before you go to bed. Or if you really want to write that book, make sure that when you open your laptop, the first thing you see is a half-finished sentence from your next chapter.

What we know for sure: the Dunning-Kruger Effect

You must know at least one person who is incompetent in a field but incorrectly sees him/herself as the best performer. The bad driver who believes they're a good driver, the humorless friend who thinks they know what's funny, and the person in the pub who has never held public office but thinks they'd make a terrific politician. After all, how hard can it be? How is it that people can be so overoptimistic in assessing their own potential? According to social psychologists David Dunning and Justin Kruger, it is because they are too ignorant in these domains to know otherwise. They call this the "Dunning-Kruger Effect", a bias we all have in failing to recognize our own incompetence. In a series of experiments, Dunning and Kruger tested students in the areas of humor, grammar, and logic and compared each student's test results with the same student's estimate of how well they had scored. The results were hilarious if you think of it. Those who scored the lowest had vastly overestimated their scores, while those who did best had slightly underestimated their performance. As we become more knowledgeable, we also become more aware of the gaps in our knowledge and as a result we display lower confidence. Similarly, incompetent people don't recognize their lack of competence and fail to recognize the competence of others. So it seems that ignorance is a bliss. But together with big dreams, it can become a deadly cocktail. Imagine that you have a big dream, but you're not aware that you don't have the competencies to achieve it. It won't happen to you, you think? It happens to all of us. We've been jury members for countless PhD proposals, entrepreneurial pitches and the whole shebang. And we continue to be amazed by how often people present ideas for which they just don't have the right skillset or background (how on earth can you develop a new app for healthcare if you don't know anything about healthcare?). Not having the competencies (yet) should not in itself be a dealbreaker. There's a lot that you can learn. But having a big dream and being unaware of your incompetence is setting yourself up for failure.

Kruger, J. and D. Dunning. (2000). Unskilled and Unaware of It: How Difficulties in Recognizing One's Own Incompetence Lead to Inflated Self-Assessments. *Journal of Personality and Social Psychology,* 77 (6), 1121-1134.

The sweet spot between ambition, optimism, and hubris

Dreaming big is a double-edged sword. We all know the story of Icarus who wanted to fly towards the sun but only got burned. It's about finding the sweet spot between having healthy ambition, the optimism that you can do it and the humility to know that it's going to take hard work. Paul Bulcke, chairman of Nestlé, put it like this when we talked to him about finding this balance: 'You have to believe in yourself. Don't diminish yourself. You don't always need to have all the answers before you start, but you need the inner trust that you will figure them out along the way.' That inner trust does not need to be based on arrogance.

It's about finding the sweet spot between having healthy ambition, the optimism that you can do it and the humility to know that it's going to take hard work.

Mette Lykke, CEO of Too Good To Go, echoes that sentiment: 'I learned early in my career as a management consultant that you can achieve a lot if you put a few smart and hard-working people in a room for a few days to work on a problem. Now at Too Good To Go we have really big goals. But that does not mean we have all the answers of how to do that already. But we'll figure it out. Whenever we're at a roadblock and we stumble upon an issue, I then think 'ok, we don't know how to solve this yet, but we also haven't put some people with brainpower on it for a few days yet, and once we do that surely something will come out that will help us forward.' That kind of confidence has been very helpful.'

The inequality of dreaming

You can accomplish anything if you put your mind to it. Really? If someone tells you that, then they're talking rubbish. We're only 1.63m, and unlike the 1.93m Emma Meesseman, we will never win a WNBA finals Most Valuable Player Award, no matter how hard we work and no matter how much we "trust the process". In fact, if being great at basketball had been our moonshot project, it would probably have resulted in a giant disappointment. So, we need to talk about inequality. Because, just like mother nature did not bless us with the head start of long limbs in order to become a world-class basketball player, not everybody in the world starts with the same advantages. Even when it comes to dreaming, not everyone gets a license to dream. Structural inequality is real, and bias is also real. So how can you turn things in your favor?

It's the question that motivated Harvard professor Laura Huang to find out how you can find your edge, even when your starting position is way behind. As the daughter of Taiwanese immigrants to the United States, Laura was not predestined to make it to Harvard. Not as a student, and certainly not as a professor. But she made it her life's work to investigate the biases that people encounter, and how they can overcome them, so that they can allow their hard work to work harder for them. In her words: 'People generally underestimate two things: how hard it is to get your foot in the door as an outsider (whatever "outsider" means to you), and how wide doors are open once you're on the inside.' Laura's hard work certainly paid off, as it was her original research and unique viewpoint, garnered from being an outsider all of her life, that got her a foot in the door.

Don't be discouraged when the cards are not stacked in your favor. 'Dream enormously big, and work backwards to figure out how to get there.' These are the word of Sinéad Burke, the first little person to grace the cover of Vogue. She is on a mission to make the fashion world more inclusive. A front row fixture now at major fashion shows, she's succeeding in just that. So we live in a world where a determined and hardworking 3-foot-5-inch tall woman can become an international fashion icon. Maybe we should start this basketball career after all?

Take it from us

If someone had told us 20 years ago that we'd be a dean and a professor, we would have had a good laugh about it. And that's something we have in common with many people we talked to. Very few believed that they were destined to become what they did.

It's ok if you don't have your life's ambition spelled out just yet. You may already have figured out that you won't become a ballerina or novelist. Plenty of us make it all the way to adulthood — maybe even decades into a career — without really knowing what we want to do with our lives. And even if you don't know yet how you'll do it all, trust yourself to figure it out as you go along. But no matter what your dream is, don't dismiss it. It's a cliché as big as a house, but as clichés go there's always some truth to it. Rome wasn't built in a day. But it was built. So just get on with it. Dream the impossible dreams. And do something every day that takes you one step further on the journey.

Don't attribute your small successes along the way to sheer luck. Success is a self-fulfilling prophecy. The more you believe that you will succeed, the more you will succeed. Every step of the way, aim a little higher than you think is possible. Always dream a little bigger than you dare and you will do more than you think you are capable of. Just like a baby learns to crawl by wanting to get to a toy that is just out of reach, aim for those opportunities that are just out of reach. You may find a way to get there anyway, with persistence and hard work. Be aware that, as the saying goes: 'Opportunity is missed by most people because it is dressed in overalls and looks like hard work.' Now that our first chapter is done, time to pour ourselves that coffee!

Clap along
if you
know what
happiness
is to you.

2 Go for happiness

The myth: happiness is painless

Don't think that money does everything or you are going to end up doing everything for money.

Voltaire

You spend an inordinate amount of your life at work. Just add it all up. Let's take a conservative ballpark estimate: 8 hours a day for 5 days a week for 48 weeks a year for 40 years, which adds up to a whopping 76,800 hours. What do you want to spend these hours doing?

Surely you would prefer your work-life to be more than just a necessary evil that allows you to get on with your real life as soon as you leave work? After all, work is part of life. But what makes it worthwhile for you? Is it the money? The status? The excitement? The routine or the lack of a routine? The fun you have with your colleagues? Doing something you enjoy? What is it that makes your heart beat faster? What is it that you're really searching for?

People will tell you to follow your passion. Do what you love, and the money will follow. It's almost like a fulfilling life awaits you if only you can detect the passions you were born with. We are not among those people. We are advocates of pursuing happiness. Because you will never flourish if you are not happy with what you do. Whatever happiness means to you. Money, the conventional wisdom says, doesn't buy happiness. If you are truly unhappy at work, you are miserable for more than a third of your life. Is the comfort or that money really worth it? There is clearly more to happiness than meets the eye. You can't be happy unless you're unhappy sometimes. Understanding yourself, the good and the bad sides, is essential in your pursuit of happiness. So clap along if you know what happiness is to you.

Follow your passion?

"Follow your passion." That advice assumes that you know what your passion is, and that your passion is (pre)fixed and will not change. Do you believe that is true? Once a science nut, always a science nut. You're truly passionate about human resource management, so there's no way you'll ever become fascinated by finance, right? If that's what you believe, think about what that implies. It means that you can only have a limited number of strong interests in your life, and once you find them there is little reason to explore other things. If you believe that passions are fixed, you probably also believe that your passions should provide constant motivation and inspiration. Thus, engaging in them should come relatively easily, and should never feel boring, difficult or frustrating. That's a pretty high bar to set, but some people seem to easily jump over it! Take the Belgian tennis player Kim Clijsters, for example. It is abundantly clear that this 4-time grand slam tournament winner's passion has always been, and always will be, tennis. Twice she retired from it, and twice she came back. She stopped the first time at the age of only 23. Plagued by injuries and eager to start a family, she announced her retirement from tennis. But after having a daughter, she came back to win major tournaments again. She hung up her racket for good in 2012. At least, that was what everybody, including herself, thought. But the urge to play tennis again at the highest level proved to be too strong, and in 2020, at the age of 36, Kim Clijsters is staging a second comeback. Who knows, she may defy all odds and add a 5th grand slam title to her list of victories. Commenting on the hard work that she's doing to get back to the top level, she said: 'I'm surprised how, at times when I'm going through a rough practice, how easy it is for me to stick with it and to fight through it and to push through it.' Now if that isn't passion, then what is?!

Keep in mind that passion can develop over time.

However, it's dangerous to think that passion only manifests itself in this way. Because even if you're truly passionate about something, there will be days when you're just not feeling it. And if you don't really know yet what your passion is, don't despair. Just keep in mind that passion can develop over time, and that gives you the opportunity to explore different areas. Overnight epiphanies are actually quite rare. For most of us, finding our purpose is a lifelong journey. Yet a life without purpose leaves us feeling unhappy and unfulfilled. Several studies have found that the feeling that one's life has meaning is positively linked to just about every aspect of our lives, including our physical health. One Harvard study showed that it even impacts how well we are still able to walk when we get older. A sense of purpose can come from many aspects in life. It can come from meaningful work, or from volunteering for a non-profit organization, but it can also come from a yoga session, or even from a beautiful sunset. And there is always some serendipity involved. In fact, even when you sometimes doubt whether or not what you are doing is really what you were meant to do, the chances are high that you are actually living your purpose without realizing it.

Working for money?

Working for money isn't all bad. Seeking financial security so that you can support your family is obviously a very worthy pursuit. And, for many people, it's a necessity. One in four Europeans live in poverty. And more than half of all people in poverty live in working households, with their wages unable to match their living costs. Single parents are disproportionately likely to live in poverty. So, let's face it, if you are a single mom or dad that needs to provide for three children, you may have to work double shifts or find a side hustle ... just for the money, not out of passion. We realize that this is not exactly the kind of stuff you will find in career manuals. After all, it's not a sexy message ... because it goes against the idea that we need to pursue our dreams, no matter what. The truth is that when you are barely making ends meet, finding meaning is not your top priority. And that is fine. Work doesn't have a monopoly on happiness.

There is absolutely no reason to put yourself (or others) down because you work for money. Did you know that one of the most powerful and well-known women in business, former PepsiCo CEO Indra Nooyi, worked the graveyard

There is absolutely no reason to put yourself (or others) down because you work for money.

shift (midnight to 5 a.m.) as a receptionist to earn money while getting her masters degree at Yale? Similarly, one of the richest men in Asia and a dominant figure in Hong Kong's economy, Ka-Shing, left school at the age of 15 to work in a plastics factory to support his family. And Guy Laliberté was a fire-eater before founding Cirque du Soleil. Talk about fire in the belly – literally! Such "rags-to-riches" stories may be cliché. But they do show that not every successful person was born with a silver spoon in their mouth. In fact, when you analyze the life stories of many successful people, you'll find that through extraordinary grit and perseverance (and perhaps a golden spoon of luck), many of them beat the odds.

The pursuit of happiness: finding meaning in pain

"Everything happens for a reason." Don't you hate that cliché? It may infuriate you more than it consoles you. Got dumped by your boyfriend? Failed a test? Did not get hired for your dream job? One day you'll find out that the universe had a reason for it, or so we should believe. Even more, you're supposed to turn your bad luck into something positive. "When life gives you lemons, make lemonade." This may be the last thing you feel like doing when hard times strike. But with time and perspective, you may come to realize that it's the bad times that shaped you for the better and connected you with your core.

One of our favorite leadership books ever – "True North" by Bill George and Peter Sims – debunks the myth of the superhero top executive with the charmed life, who effortlessly swoops in like a white knight to save the day.

The book describes the authentic leadership journeys of some of the world's most influential CEOs. Journeys that, without any exceptions, began with self-awareness. We're talking about a deep and authentic understanding of yourself: your life story, your crucibles, your setbacks, and your hardships. Understanding how your life story has shaped you is an essential first step in discovering your purpose. If only exploring those dark places wasn't ... so painful!

What we know for sure: happiness includes highs and lows

"Stars can't shine without darkness". Katleen read these words on a shiny bumper sticker on a shabby old car in China and couldn't stop herself from laughing out loud. Tacky words, yes. But secretly, we all love those tacky bumper stickers, don't we? It's a pity that they are out of fashion now. This sticker highlights the importance of having highs and lows. You can't be Mister or Miss Sunshine all the time. And that's also what research shows.

You can't be Mister or Miss Sunshine all the time.

Compare three individuals: Person A experiences three moments of joy in a given day, Person B experiences two moments of joy and one moment of contentment, and Person C experiences two moments of joy and one moment of anxiety. Who do you think is in the best shape? If we add together the number of positive emotions (joy and contentment) and subtract the number of negative emotions (anxiety), A and B would be equally happy, and both would be happier than C. But there is more to it. What matters besides the number of positive emotions is what is called "emodiversity": the number of different emotions you experience. The broader the range of different emotions you experience in a given time period, the higher your emodiversity. And that turns out to be a good thing. Two studies comprising more than 37,000 respondents demonstrated that people with a higher emodiversity also have better mental and physical health.

So the emodiversity of A, B, and C's emotions—the variety and relative abundance of the emotions they experience—is an independent and integral component of the human emotional ecosystem that predicts both mental and physical health. In other words, in order to be really happy you need to know what unhappiness feels like. In the same way that the sun feels warmer when it comes peeking out from behind the clouds, it's the lows that make your highs feel higher.

Quoidbach, J., J. Gruber, M. Mikolajczak, A. Kogan, I. Kotsou, and M. Norton. (2014). Emodiversity and the Emotional Ecosystem. *Journal of Experimental Psychology,* 143 (6), 2057-2066.

Pain is inevitable, suffering is optional (Haruki Murakami)

During World War II, the Austrian neurologist and psychiatrist Viktor Emil Frankl lost his entire future when his mother, father, brother, and pregnant wife were killed in the concentration camps. After the war, he wrote a book, "Man's Search for Meaning", in which he describes how he coped with his devastating losses and hardships. He explains how he convinced himself that the only thing that the Nazis could not take away from him was his freedom to choose how he responded to the horror he was subjected to. He pushed himself to think that, even in the most dehumanized, absurd, and painful situations, life has a potential meaning and that, therefore, even pain is meaningful ...

It is hard to imagine how, in the midst of such horror, anyone could be capable of identifying a purpose in life to feel positive about. While few of us have experienced anything remotely resembling the terror of a concentration camp, we all have (and will have) our own crucibles: times of adversity that test our character and that force us to develop a new sense of identity. A personal illness, the death of a loved one, a divorce, feelings of being excluded or discriminated against, etc. We all yearn for positive experiences that make us thrive, but it's often the losses, failures, and disappointments that have a deeper impact and enable us to develop a new sense of meaning.

It's often the losses, failures, and disappointments that have a deeper impact and enable us to develop a new sense of meaning.

One of the life stories described in "True North" is the story of Starbucks CEO Howard Schultz. He describes that he had a very difficult and painful childhood. His father had a work accident, leaving him injured and unable to work. He lost his job and health insurance, leaving the family in extreme poverty. Throughout most of his childhood, Howard was angry with what he then saw as his underachieving, irresponsible father. It was only later that he came to realize that his father was the victim of a poorly functioning healthcare system. This insight allowed him to reconcile with his father and with his past, and made Starbucks one of the pioneering companies in providing healthcare for all workers, even the part-timers. Going back to his difficult roots also helped Howard Schultz to grow the Starbucks business. He grew up in Brooklyn during the sixties, which was a poor but diverse neighborhood with lots of Italian immigrants, where a typical Friday evening entailed sitting around a table with all kinds of people to enjoy an Italian meal. When he made a trip to Italy later in life, he found that the Milanese coffee shops were gathering places in just the same way. He wanted Starbucks to be a place like that, and, eventually, he wanted places like that to exist in communities all over the world. The rest is history.

What we know for sure: self-reflection makes you happier

Self-reflection helps us to lead a more meaningful life. But many of us hate it. We find reflection difficult, troublesome, or just a waste of time. In one study, people were given the option either to spend 15 minutes alone with their thoughts and feelings or to shock themselves with a 9-volt battery. For 15 minutes, the research team left the participants alone in a lab room in which they could push a button and shock themselves if they wanted to. The results were startling. Even though all of the participants had previously stated that they would pay money to avoid being shocked with electricity, a majority chose to shock themselves rather than just sit there quietly and think. Clearly, not all of us are ready for daily meditation!

Yet, reflection does have proven benefits. It allows us to pause amid the chaos, to reframe our experiences, and to find (or create) meaning in what we do. It can even help us to appreciate our jobs and develop an overall sense of purpose in life. In one study, commuters were prompted to use their commute for self-reflection. As a result they felt happier, more productive, and less burned out than those who didn't.

Ashforth, B. E., and Kreiner, G. E. (1999). "How can you do it?": Dirty work and the challenge of constructing a positive identity. Academy of management Review, 24(3), 413-434.

Ashford, S. J., and DeRue, D. S. (2012). Developing as a leader: The power of mindful engagement. *Organizational Dynamics, 41*(2), 146-154.

Gino, F., B. Staats, J. M. Jachimowicz, J. Lee and J. I. Menges. (2017). Reclaim Your Commute. *Harvard Business Review,* July 2017.

Wilson, T. D., D. A. Reinhard, E. C. Westgate, D. T. Gilbert, N. Ellerbeck, C. Hahn, C. L. Brown and A. Shaked. (2014). Just Think: The Challenges of the Disengaged Mind. *Science,* 345, 6192, 75-77.

Get off the treadmill

The stories of Dr Frankl and Howard Schultz highlight how reflecting on one's life story can help you to find meaning and a sense of purpose, and deep happiness as a result. Reflection shouldn't just be something that you do around New Year—or when you are in trouble. Why not follow S'well CEO Sarah Kauss (or President Truman) and keep a journal. Similarly, LinkedIn CEO Jeff Weiner reports that he spends between 90 and 120 minutes each day reflecting. After all, didn't Blaise Pascal point out that 'All of humanity's problems come from man's inability to sit quietly in a room alone'? So you may need to step off the treadmill of life every once in a while, to stand still and consider if you're still running in the right direction.

You may need to step off the treadmill of life every once in a while, to stand still and consider if you're still running in the right direction.

Katleen remembers: 'Last year I was diagnosed with an autoimmune disorder that, among other things, results in unpredictable hair loss (I hate to say it, but yes: baldness). It also came with a less common side-effect: every now and then I look like elephant woman. Nothing serious really, but somehow it made me upset. I remember doing a silent walk with a group of participants in the UK ... something that I would have deeply enjoyed in the past, now left me in great distress. I did the entire walk with my hand on my head to cover the bald spots. Of course, I tried not to be a drama queen and joked about how I'd become bald and beautiful. But inside I felt quite shocked. Later I learned that one of the causes that can trigger a flare is stress. But how was that possible, I hardly ever experienced stress? Or did I? In retrospect, I have to admit that I was addicted to being busy. And in the process, I was telling myself to be strong. After all, I had no reason to complain. Today, I feel that this disorder was a gift that came at the right time. It pushed me to slow down a bit ... and to reflect on what really matters. Reflection isn't about doing less. It's about pausing and listening to your true feelings. And that process allowed me to take bigger leaps and focus on what really matters. I don't think I would ever have considered writing a book, nor running my first marathon, if it hadn't been for this new, harmless companion pushing me to rethink how I was leading my life (I admit that the marathon-challenge Benoit – a former MBA-student – set, helped as well). It's actually quite ironic that a leadership professor, of all people, had to learn about the importance of self-reflection this way.'

Marion echoes this experience: 'When I told my American colleagues that I was going to leave the US and go back to Belgium, they thought I was insane. And for sure they did not hide the fact that they felt this was a clear step back. Basically, I would not be able to achieve a successful academic career after this move, in their eyes, and while being polite and gracious, I could hear their disappointment and disapproval in every comment. To be honest, it hurt. I had worked so hard to secure this position. It had taken me months of introspection to come to terms with the decision to leave. But I had to admit to myself that I was simply not happy. I joined Vlerick Business School, the place where I had been a student, met my best friends, and that had changed me as a person. It was a decision of the heart, more than the brain. And in the end, what others questioned to be a good career move, turned out to be the best life decision I ever made.'

Take it from us

Take it from us, work is about more than money. At least, it can be about much more if you let it, and be a tremendous source of happiness. Students often ask us the important "What should I do with my life?" question. And we admit that, early on in our careers, this was also one of the big questions on our own minds ... after all, you don't want to find out that you followed the wrong path. Until you figure out that there may not be a wrong path, as your destination is not set. It is the journey itself that matters and the important thing is to enjoy it.

Passions are dynamic and evolving. So over the years we have stopped trying to find "our passion". In a way, we have come to appreciate the concept of purpose, in the same way that we have come to appreciate the concept of "true love": you find it when you stop looking for it. In other words, when you stop evaluating every possibility as the potential "one", and when you stop forcing a match on yourself, it might actually bring you one step closer to your purpose. Because most of the answers you may be looking for are already stored inside you. Just stop and think.

Only you can decide what success means to you.

3 Carve your own path

The myth: the only way is up

Success is not final, failure is not fatal, it's the courage to continue that counts.

Winston Churchill

You made it! Only, what is "it" and how do you get there? The classic way to think about work and success is as a ladder which you dutifully climb until you've arrived at the top. We assume that if we work hard, we will progress and move up that ladder. And we also think that if we do not have an upward trajectory, then somehow we must have failed or done something terribly wrong. If only it were that simple! But also, how boring does that sound! Luckily, life will certainly hand you some unexpected twists and turns. And you will also probably redefine the idea of success a couple of times.

Because as the world around us changes, and existing industries and companies are disrupted, careers will be disrupted as well. Careers with a straight line to the top may become a rare phenomenon, and certainly not the only route to success. Sheryl Sandberg, COO of Facebook, argues that instead of using the analogy of a ladder, we should use the analogy of a jungle gym. On a ladder, you can only go up or down. But on a jungle gym, you

On a jungle gym, you can take multiple routes to reach the end.

can take multiple routes to reach the end (because there is not really a "top"). And those routes go up, down, and sideways. So get ready to swing along, slide down, and climb back up!

You decide what success means

What is success really? Is it when you can finally drive that Porsche? Is it when you are famous? Is it when you can retire with enough money in the bank to live happily ever after? Or is it when you wake up every day excited to get started? When you can afford to take a sabbatical? You know what: it's entirely up to you. Only you can decide whether or not you are successful. Your definition of success is deeply personal and will most definitely change over time. In the early stages of your career, you will most likely measure it in terms of having new challenges every day, first wins, recognition, and results. And also by the small "material" tokens of success: your amount of travel abroad, your business card, and your job title. As you move forward, you typically start caring more about your quality of life, financial stability, good health, and quality relationships.

To many, climbing the ladder of success usually means one thing: getting to the top! But it's a myth that success means that you need to become a boss at work. The beauty of careers is that, behind every objective career success, there is also the subjective feeling that comes with it. If your definition of success is just an endless list of objective perks, such as your pay or benefits, then that's your choice. But it may not be very rewarding. So make sure that you frequently reflect on whether or not your objective and subjective career successes are still in check. Because that's the secret to having it all. Driving that Porsche in an attempt to keep up with Joneses, while feeling like a wreck on the inside ... well, if that makes you happy. But who wants to keep up with the Joneses anyway?

It's your road to travel

Sometimes everything just falls into place.

Finally, you get the success you truly deserve. You have put in the long hours, conquered many challenges, and finally you're rewarded for your efforts. For you, success could mean becoming a director, finally seeing your business flourish, or landing that investment. But it could also involve a big athletic accomplishment, writing your first bestselling book, or going viral with your blog. Of course, your success also comes with some extra perks and privileges: more visibility, higher pay, maybe a new car, or a move to a new office. And it also comes with the biggest perk of all: a whole lot of extra responsibility. The taste of success is sweet. But there's this daunting feeling creeping in. You've done everything that everyone expected from you, but there's this little voice that you can't seem to shut up. It's asking you: is this "it"?

When you move in a certain direction, there will always be two choices ahead of you. One choice will be the conventional path. The route that almost everybody else is taking. When you study law, you try to get an intern position at a prestigious law firm. Way ahead of you is the golden trophy of becoming a partner at said firm. When you study medicine, you're supposed to specialize and develop your own practice. When you study economics, your destiny is to join a big consulting firm, where you can climb up the ladder to partnership. Or you join a company, at the bottom of the totem pole, as a trainee. And work hard to climb all the way up. You get the drill. Your life is laid out in front of you. And it's not a bad life. But it's a life that was engineered for you by others. When it fits you like a glove, by all means go for it! But when it doesn't, it's up to you to make up your own mind. You can count on it. Every step of the way, there will be people around you who will tell you to stay on the conventional path.

But you should know that there is always the other option. The option to go off the beaten path. Against the grain. Rest assured that when you do that, people will tell you that you are crazy. But what if you're not? What if you're a genius? Because going off the beaten path will give you a unique profile and unique competencies. It will develop you into a lateral thinker, who can take ideas from one domain and connect them with ideas from another domain. And it will give you a unique set of competencies, which will set you apart from everyone else. And then you're really onto something. Quoting Coco Chanel: 'If you want to be irreplaceable, you have to be different.'

'If you want to be irreplaceable, you have to be different.'

Marion recounts: 'When I graduated as a chemical engineer, all of my friends joined chemical companies and went into manufacturing or R&D. That was simply the standard thing to do, and there were plenty of options for each of us. But I just knew it wasn't for me. I chose to do an additional Master's, with a specialization in marketing. My fellow engineers were flabbergasted. Marketing? For an engineer? What a waste! And when I graduated from that Master's program, I chose to go into academia to pursue a PhD. Again, I got a similar reaction. All of my marketeer friends aimed for a fancy job as brand manager at a multinational company, whereas I went for the nerdy path of research. I'm sure they wished me well, but at the same time couldn't fathom why on earth I wanted to do this. And indeed, for the next couple of years, I was behind my desk and knee-deep in data and papers, while they rocked a much more glamorous life. But I loved the pursuit of deep knowledge and the absolute freedom of the life of a researcher.'

Katleen had a similar experience: 'When I joined Vlerick, some of my peers were startled. I even received an e-mail from a former high school friend, who asked me what had happened to me. After all, I was a psychologist who had been super engaged in volunteering activities for Oxfam. Wasn't I supposed to stand up for the weakest in society instead of joining a business school focused on educating privileged business people? Didn't this decision go against everything I stood for? His words hurt because I had been asking myself some of those same questions. But somehow I felt it was what I had to do. Later, I realized that what my gut had been telling me was right all along. Granted, business can be held co-accountable for many societal problems like climate change and inequality. But business also has the power to create prosperity, to provide meaning and solve many of those same societal challenges. I still can't think of a more fulfilling purpose for myself than researching and teaching about how this can be done.'

When you don't make it your way

Sometimes everything seems to fall apart.

You didn't get that promotion. Or maybe you wanted to be an entrepreneur, but you ended up as a wantrepreneur. You put in all the hard work for those Olympic Games, but then you got injured. Or perhaps you've just "been there, done that".

An unrealized dream can be disheartening. After all, no one likes to hear that they didn't have what it takes. But it happens all the time. Most of us work under the assumption that our efforts will ultimately lead to career advancement. But the reality is that, more often than not, we don't always get what we want (or deserve). Take it from us, an unrealized aspiration shouldn't be the end of the world. And it will certainly not be the end of your career. Your first reaction after missing out on a promotion may be to hit the job market and start sending out your resume. Or, if your catering business doesn't take off, you might want to become a gardener instead. But just because you suffered one (or multiple) major setback, you don't need to jump ship. Many people have been overlooked for the success they deserved. And many of them have come back stronger and more successful. In situations like this, it's important to keep things in perspective and realize that your career (and life) is bigger than this one event.

Take it from us, an unrealized aspiration shouldn't be the end of the world. And it will certainly not be the end of your career.

You never know, but when that one door closes, another may really open (as much as you may want to kick the person who tells you that when you're still recovering from the blow of failure). Defeat may contain a kernel of success. That was certainly the case for Arianna Huffington. Born in Greece as Arianna Stasinopoulou, she managed to obtain a scholarship to attend Cambridge University. After graduating, she went into journalism, moved to the US in her early thirties, and became a bestselling biography writer. She married politician Michael Huffington and, through him, became more and more involved in politics, to the extent that she even ran for governor of California. Up against another outsider candidate by the name of Arnold Schwarzenegger, her campaign was not a success, and she suffered a very public defeat. For the intellectual Huffington, losing a political campaign against a muscular actor was definitely not her finest hour. But it was by trying to rally support on a limited budget that she learned about the power of the internet. Soon afterwards, while traditional newspapers were still figuring out what to make of the internet, Arianna created the Huffington Post and rewrote the rules of print media for a digital world. The Huffington Post's business model was not based on the idea that that a newspaper should tightly control its content through its editorial staff. Rather, the idea was for it to function as a curator, bringing together material from other channels, as well as from bloggers and opinion makers who submitted their material in return for the exposure. It quickly became one of the most visited internet sites in the world, providing an alternative news source with all content freely accessible. And while most newspapers were struggling with declining readership and adapting themselves to a digital world, the Huffington Post flourished and was ultimately sold to AOL for $315 million. Arianna created the Huffington Post at the age of 55, defying all expectations that a successful tech entrepreneur must be young and male, and simultaneously showing that it's never too late to reinvent yourself.

What we know for sure: what doesn't kill you does make you stronger

In a groundbreaking study that was published in *Nature,* researchers investigated the career trajectory of young scientists. They compared those who applied for a prestigious grant and got it with those that applied but didn't get it. They were interested in finding out the consequences of an early-career setback involving not getting this important grant. To make sure that the researchers did not compare apples and oranges, they selected a sample containing 2 groups. The first group contained those young scientists whose score was just above what was needed to obtain the grant. They called those the "narrow wins". The second group contained those scientists who scored just below what was required to obtain a grant. They called these the "near misses". The two groups were not different in any other way, except for the fact that they either barely obtained the grant or barely didn't. The first group started their scientific career with a clear leg-up, while the second group started their career with a clear disappointment. What did this failure mean for their future career? Not surprisingly, the near misses were more likely to give up and quit science altogether. But the ones who persisted turned out to do really well later on. In fact, over the next decade they produced more impactful work than the narrow wins and became more successful.

Wang, J., B. Jones, and D. Wang. (2019). Early-Career Setback and Future Career Impact. *Nature*, 10, 4331.

Up is not the only way

If you look closely at the careers of people you admire, you'll find out that these careers often involve a lot of zigzagging: moving laterally, jumping organizational levels, taking steps back, and taking leaps forward. It's ok to take a detour every now and then. Many people needlessly worry that taking a step sideward, and especially a step backward, may derail their careers. But sometimes, taking a step back will take you further. Acknowledging when you need to take a step back can be hard. We invest such a large portion of our time in our jobs and to feeling like we're on the right track. But, which track are we really on?

What looks like a step back may actually turn out to be a step forward. Paul Bulcke shares: 'When I was in charge of the Portugal market for Nestlé, which I really enjoyed, I was asked quite soon to leave and take up the Czech market instead. It didn't feel like a promotion at the time. The market was only half the size of the Portuguese. We were in a complex joint venture situation. I had mixed feelings about taking it on. When I expressed these mixed feelings to my boss, he said 'I'm not giving you a job, I'm giving you my trust'. So I took it on and it turned out to be a fantastic experience, and a great stepping stone toward becoming responsible for the German market later on.'

Sometimes, taking a step back will take you further.

Make space for serendipity

Once you accept the fact that your career journey will look more like a zigzag path than a well-planned straight road, you can open your mind to a diverse set of possible routes. Maybe there are a few highways to success (such as putting your work first), but, in addition to those highways, there are many alternatives, and certainly prettier and more enjoyable routes to success. Embracing that imperfection and unpredictability creates space for the scenic route. If you take that one, you leave room for chance encounters and projects that, while they seem to sidetrack you, enrich you in other ways. And that always pays dividends. Marion recounts: 'A little while ago I was asked to write a column for the *Financial Times.* And because it was the *Financial Times,* I said yes, even though I did not really have the time for it. I remember working on the piece while on the beach in Ibiza on a birthday celebration weekend with friends. While they were all relaxing, I was working against the deadline and struggling with the concept, cursing myself for having said yes to this assignment. The format dictated that I would write about a real-life person (historical or current). I really wanted a female protagonist and landed on Arianna Huffington, whose many accomplishments and outspoken public profile had always fascinated me. Much to my surprise, she wrote me an email the day after the column was published. One thing led to another, and a few months later I was on a plane to visit the headquarters of her new company in New York, and spent a few hours talking to her. It was just a delight to experience this, and I learned a lot from this encounter. But it would have never happened had I not said yes to writing this column.'

You don't need to have everything planned. Serendipity plays a role, if you let it. You may even become the CEO of a social impact company. That's the true story of how Mette Lykke got involved with the company Too Good To Go, of which she is now CEO. Too Good To Go is an app that connects users with unsold food from a variety of shops and restaurants, which you can then pick up at a reduced price. The company's goal is to save 1 billion meals from going to waste and to create more awareness around food waste and its impact on the environment. Mette shares: 'I was in a bus out of Copenhagen and I started chatting with the woman next to me. She showed me the Too Good To Go app, and I really liked it. She knew the founders and we agreed she would introduce me. I got in touch and asked if I could help out. It turns out they were looking to spar with someone who had worked with apps (which I had experience with in my first start-up), and that's how I got involved. When I first saw the app, I intuitively felt it was a great thing, I've always felt bad throwing food out. But then I read about the history of food waste and that we actually throw out a third of our food and how this contributes to the climate issue. I just really wanted to contribute. One thing led to another and today I'm a shareholder and CEO of Too Good To Go.'

You don't need to have everything planned.

The way down

If you feel that moving forward in your career means climbing your way up the ladder, then it also requires you to think about the way down. Paul Bulcke says: ‘People always talk about how to go up. But actually, what you should equally be prepared for is the way down. Just like a mountaineer needs to practice and prepare to get up the mountain, but also to get back down safely. The mission has only succeeded when you’re back on ground zero. Even if you’re a high-powered CEO of a big company, you will not stay that forever. There will be a day when you’ll step down from that role. Can you still be happy then? And throughout the journey, there are always ups and downs. You need to prepare for the downs and even be able to enjoy them. Your ability to fall and then stand up again is what matters.’

Take it from us

Many people think that their careers can only succeed if they take the straight road to the top. The reality is that the most worthwhile journeys take some twists and turns. Sometimes the best long-term decision even requires a backward move. And if, for you, the only way is up, then remember this: what goes up ultimately must come down.

Is the perfect job out there?

4 Embrace the imperfection

The myth: the perfect job is out there

If you want the rainbow,
you gotta put up with the rain.

Dolly Parton

So, there you are, married with children, maybe a cat or a dog, and a nice house with a garden to top it all off. Or perhaps you are (un)happily single, enjoying a life without kids, sharing custody, or taking care of a sick relative. Maybe you are dreaming of travelling the world or actually doing it ... or all of the above. And then there is work. Perhaps you are still one of the happy (or unhappy) few with a so-called "9 to 5" type of job. Or maybe you are working in a flexible type of work arrangement, either by choice or out of necessity. No matter how standard or non-standard your life looks from the outside, it will surely sometimes feel ginormously complicated to you on the inside.

So many options! So many choices! Should you say yes to that project abroad? Should you quit and go freelance? Should you fulfill that eternal dream of being an entrepreneur and finally do something about that business idea that you and your friends are always brainstorming during long chatty (& boozy) evenings? Or should you just stay put and persevere where you are? Your choices and options are endless, and that is both the agony and the ecstasy of today's labor market. You choose, you lose?

The paradox of choice

You know that feeling you get when you try to decide what to have from the restaurant's menu? The penne al ragu sounds enticing, but you can also smell the pizza coming out of the wood brick oven and it smells just divine. And just when you put your order in for a pizza margherita, you see a bubbling hot lasagna being served at the table next to you, and it instantly hits you. That's what you're really craving!

Having choices does not necessarily make you happy. That is called the paradox of choice. We tend to think that it's a good thing to have more options. And that's true when the choice you need to make remains manageable. Choosing between 3 things? Easy-peasy. But choosing between 10? That's another thing. Too many options can leave you feeling paralyzed. How do you know what is right for you, right now? You keep on overthinking and overanalyzing, and ultimately you can't make up your mind. And once you do, there is always that lingering feeling of 'What if..?' Even after swiping right and making your catch, you can't help but think of the other fish in the sea!

The perennial search for perfection leaves you never feeling fully content. The reality is that very often there is no way of knowing what the right option is for you. Just pick one and make something of it. As our colleague Marc Buelens would say: 'Make your choice, and then love your choice.'

What we know for sure: even though perfection does not exist, we want it more than ever

You expect a lot, from yourself mostly but also from others. Perfection is what you are going for, and nothing less. If that sounds familiar, you are not alone. A recent study investigated whether perfectionism is more prevalent today than it was in the past. Over a 27-year period, the study brings together 164 data samples of college students in the UK, US, and Canada. And the conclusions are very clear: we are more perfectionist today than we were in the past. That is true for 3 different types of perfectionism. The first is called "self-oriented perfectionism", which is about the high and unrealistic expectations you have for yourself. A second type of perfectionism is about what you feel others expect of you. This is called "socially prescribed" perfectionism which basically is about the pressure you feel to fulfil the high expectations that others have for you. You may believe your social context is excessively demanding, that others judge you harshly, and that you must display perfection to secure approval. These days, when the likes you amass on social media can quickly become a measure of self-worth, this type of others-induced perfectionism is especially rampant. But we also become less and less tolerant for others' deficiencies. The third type of perfectionism is "other-oriented" perfectionism, which means that you impose unrealistic standards on those around you and evaluate others critically.

Even though we know perfection does not exist, and we may never achieve it, we do expect it more and more, from ourselves and from others, and we also increasingly feel that others expect it from us. Perfectionism is at an all-time high with college students, putting unrealistic burdens on themselves and their surroundings.

Curran, T and Hill, A. (2019). Perfectionism Is Increasing Over Time: A Meta-Analysis of Birth Cohort Differences From 1989 to 2016. *Psychological Bulletin, vol 145(4)*, 410-429.

Is the perfect job out there?

The idea that the perfect job is out there somewhere, waiting for you like a professional soulmate, is a dangerous illusion. The prince on the white horse only exists in fairy tales. Just as you cannot expect perfection from your significant other (you may try!), you cannot demand perfection from your job. You can spend your whole life trying to find the perfect professional role. But every time you feel like you are getting really close, it will disappear like a fata morgana.

The prince on the white horse only exists in fairy tales.

It's a lesson that our friend Sam had to learn the hard way. From the outside, he appears to have a wildly exciting job, which many people would love to have. He often travels to interesting places around the globe, in order to meet up with his company's local teams. And yet, to him it all feels like endless suffering. Flights get delayed. Crossing time zones on a regular basis messes up his biorhythms. He's sick and tired of hotel food, which is the same almost anywhere. And he misses meeting people from other companies. He didn't always feel this way though. The job he had before this one had been much more local. And he had enjoyed the client contact he had at the time. But then he got antsy from being confined to one region. So he had been very happy to move up to the global level and join the internal consulting team that he was now part of. But now the glory of it had kind of faded. Actually, his previous job at another company was probably the best one he ever had. The travelling had been manageable, and he had been at the forefront of interesting client projects. But the company was small, and in the end he had felt that his growth opportunities were limited. Actually, when you think of it, Sam's career has been comprised of a series of jobs about which he was always enthusiastic at first, until the downsides became apparent, and then he would lose his steam.

Should he just stick it out now? Or move on to the next opportunity in the continuous pursuit of the perfect job? Maybe the answer is neither. Maybe Sam should consider becoming a job crafter. Job crafting is a way of redefining your job so that it becomes more "you". It's about you steering your career and molding your job in such a way that it matches not only your passions and desires, but also your very practical needs and wants. It basically allows you to turn a job within a company into "your own thing" ... and the good news is that this is a process that is entirely driven by you, not by your company and not by your boss. Job crafters take matters into their own hands, so that even if their job is not perfect, it becomes closer to their ideal image than it was before. And even if you can't change your job, you can change the way you think about it. Just emulate the janitor of NASA. The story goes that John F. Kennedy visited the NASA space center and saw a janitor carrying a broom and cleaning the hallways. He walked

> Job crafting is a way of redefining your job so that it becomes more "you".

over and asked what he was doing. The janitor responded: 'Mr. President, I'm helping put a man on the moon.'

What we know for sure: instead of finding the perfect job, craft it

Most of us assume that if we dislike our job, our only option is to leave and find a "better" opportunity elsewhere. But there's research that shows that there is another option. It's called job crafting, and it's about making the most of the job you already have. It's about you defining your job, instead of your job defining you. Every job has boundaries. But, as it turns out, many of these boundaries are mental fences. By moving them around, you can change either the nature of your job or the way you think about it. Job crafting is about making subtle but significant changes to what you do at work. The best thing about job crafting is that you don't need your supervisor's approval to craft your job. It's entirely your choice, your responsibility.

You can craft your job in three different ways: by changing your tasks, your relationships, and/or your own perceptions of the work that you do. You can change the boundaries of your tasks either by taking on more or fewer tasks, or by putting more emphasis on certain parts of your work. For example, the marketing assistant who volunteers to be part of a social media taskforce. Or the sales manager who enjoys coaching young trainees and makes an extra effort to follow up with them. You can also craft your job by changing the nature of your interactions with others. For example, the project manager who makes a point of having lunch with a different colleague every day.

Or the supply chain trainee who craves to learn from the more senior staffers and does this by giving them a weekly update report and then asking them for feedback. Finally, you can also change your own perceptions of your work, by reframing the work that you do in order to come to terms with what it entails. For example, someone who does "dirty work" and who tries to find meaning in their work by reframing it. Blake Ashforth, who studies how people find meaning in dirty work, describes a gravedigger who is often asked the question about how he copes with the reality that he has to bury people every single day. The gravedigger responds that he sees a funeral as being one of the most natural and essential things in the world, and it's something that he enjoys contributing to. One of the stories we read in the newspaper is the one concerning Ingeborg, who is a prosector. No idea what they do? Neither did we, but apparently a prosector is someone who dissects cadavers for the illustration of anatomical lectures. It's the type of job very few people could ever envision themselves doing, let alone be something that they aspire to do. However, Ingeborg does not see herself as someone who prosects bodies; she prefers to call it 'taking care of the bodies of people who donated their body to medical science. We are very grateful to the donors. What they do is necessary and valuable. Without their donation, our students would not be able to learn about anatomy, nor would surgeons be able to learn new procedures. Not everyone would want to do my work. But the idea that my job actually means something, really fulfils me.'

Research shows that many people, and particularly millennials, expect to "get" a meaningful job. But examples like this show that meaning is not something that you just "get", it also requires an effort from your side.

Wrzesniewski, A. and J. E. Dutton. (2001). Crafting Your Job: Revisioning Employees as Active Crafters of Their Work. *Academy of Management Review*, 26 (2), 179-201.

Should I stay or should I go?

Let's be clear. No job is perfect, and it's better to just accept that than to frustrate yourself in the perennial search for the ideal one. Let's face it. You may be passionate about your job as sales manager, but still hate doing your expense notes. You may really like your role as team leader, but really dread budget season. Nevertheless, there may be times when you really ask yourself whether it is time to move on.

You might get stuck because you've seen it all before. Oftentimes perfectly smart and talented people—even superior performers—get stuck. You'll know exactly what makes you feel stuck: the lockstep of narrow expertise, unstimulating work, and a flat learning curve. In those situations, you might tell yourself "Give it some time, it will get better". Or perhaps you'll make some deep reflections about how to become unstuck. And these things may help you to feel less stuck. At least for a while. According to career expert Herminia Ibarra, it can also be a pitfall to overthink or minimize the situation. Sometimes you need a real change. And that may be very hard. When you find yourself in this situation, you basically have two options: either you start crafting your job so that it fits you again or you take a leap. So the answer is simple: you act. A feeling like this doesn't always just fade or disappear. If, after 2 years of feeling stuck, the feeling is still there, it will probably stay. That little voice in the back of your head will only shout louder. So sometimes you just need a little more action. After all, you don't want to look back with regrets.

Perhaps it's helpful to ask yourself these questions in order to identify those red flags that should urge you to pack up and leave. The first question to ask yourself in the "should I stay or should I go?" dilemma is whether or not you're still learning. As Tim van Hauwermeiren, CEO of Argenx, told us in his keynote speech for the opening of the academic year at Vlerick: 'Care more about your learning curve than your salary curve.' Or, paraphrasing Confucius: 'If you are the smartest person in the room, leave that room.' The upward trajectory of your career is measured by how much you develop and learn.

Sometimes you need a real change. The answer is simple: you act.

Secondly, ask yourself whether or not your current job fits with your personal purpose and passion. Does it give you energy, or do you find your energy depleted at the end of the day? Roch Doliveux shared a very simple test: 'How do you feel when you wake up in the morning? Can you engage your brain, heart and guts in your job?' But don't forget that, just like food, passion is also often an acquired taste, which requires determination and proactivity to craft it.

A real red flag question is probably this one: "Are your core values corrupted?" Deborah told us the following story. Her previous job started out as a dream story. She had finally realized her dream of working for a rapidly growing tech company. It was a fantastic opportunity to be at the forefront of what was happening in the rapidly changing digital landscape and be part of an exciting story to build the company into a global powerhouse. As she discovered, however, the job quickly turned from a dream into a nightmare. Her direct boss turned out to be incredibly challenging to work with. Sometimes charming, but at other times a real bully. She soon started dreading their weekly update meetings, which often involved an hour of being shouted at. While her boss wanted her to lead her team with iron discipline and pressure, her own leadership style was more about empowerment and collaboration. Her breaking point came when he pushed her to fire one of her team members, even though she really appreciated the guy. Faced with the choice of either not being able to look at herself in the mirror or to resign herself, she chose the latter. Looking back, she admits 'I cannot believe I put up with this guy for so long. I should have left far sooner, but I really wanted to succeed. I had worked so hard to get to this opportunity. It was a dream job that turned into a nightmare.'

Take it from us

The perfect job does not exist. If you are one of the lucky ones and have found it, let us know. Why not think of every job you take as a stepping stone on your journey to a fulfilling, but not perfect, job? Every rose has its thorn and every job involves tasks that you despise. And, like the Little Prince in Antoine De Saint-Exupéry's book had to discover, it's the time you spend with your rose that makes your rose the most important. So spend more time on crafting the way you relate to your work, and embrace the imperfections. Because you are not perfect, and neither will your job ever be.

It's about juggling while balancing.

5 Be a juggler

The myth: to be successful, I need to "sacrifice" everything else

Be sure when you step, step with care and great tact. And remember life is a great balancing act. And will you succeed? Yes. You will indeed. 98 and 3/4 percent guaranteed. Kid, you'll move mountains.

Dr. Seuss

Success comes at a price. That seems to be common knowledge. And when success is defined in professional terms, the price you pay is in your personal life. Elon Musk famously said 'Nobody ever changed the world on 40 hours a week.' With grand ambitions come grand sacrifices, or so it seems. In an interview with the *New York Times* in 2018, Musk talked about the "excruciating" personal toll that building his company, Tesla, had on his personal life. He missed his brother's wedding, spent his entire birthday working, and would often work 120 hours a week. Sounds crazy to you? Or just the expected price of success? Social media guru Gary Vaynerchuk seems to think the latter. Want to be as successful as he is? His advice is plain and simple: 'Work harder and work faster.'

Is this really true? And what is the price you are willing to pay?

To balance or not to balance, is that the real question? About sprint races and marathons

You are ambitious. If you weren't, you probably would not be reading this book. Being ambitious, you might think that life is a combination of sprint races: the sprint race for having the coolest job, the sprint race for climbing the corporate ladder, and the sprint race for being the busiest (and thus most important) person on the planet. After all, it's called the "race to the top", so surely you need to feel as though you're running as fast as you can all the time? As exhausting as that may be. In your darkest moments, you may ask yourself the following questions. How on earth do others cope with this? How do they have both a career and a life? To start with the bottom line: if there is one thing we know for sure, it's that others are not coping nearly as well as you think they are. And actually, they may be running a different race altogether.

Charles Handy said it nicely: 'Life is a marathon, not a horse race'. He advises all of us to just opt out of races ... meaning that you should pick the long haul track, the marathon, and make sure you can last the entire distance. By setting your sights further away in the distance you can shrug off the small day-to-day victories and losses. Think about the incredible resilience that Thomas Edison showed in his endeavor to develop the light bulb. He famously said: 'I did not

By setting your sights further away in the distance you can shrug off the small day-to-day victories and losses.

fail, I just found 10,000 ways that did not work.' Imagine what would have happened if he had thought of his quest as a sprint. And did you know that J. K. Rowling, the author of the Harry Potter novels, was waitressing and on public assistance when she was writing the first book in the series—a book that also got rejected by over a dozen publishers? The only reason it got published at all was because a CEO's eight-year-old daughter begged him to.

The tricky thing with sprint races is that you get addicted to winning trophies. And endlessly competing, or the fear of not winning (or losing), may start to wear you down. But does leading a purposeful life mean that you should avoid sprint races and trophies altogether? We think not. There is no need to become the next Jean-Paul Sartre. He was awarded the Nobel Prize in 1964 but declined it, as he did with every single official honor or prize that was bestowed on him. Milestones can be important and sometimes you do deserve some credit and a little trophy for all your hard work. Go on, celebrate the small wins! And, more importantly, let the people around you celebrate with you. It's the best way to say thanks, and allows you to build the stamina to go on again. Because marathons are hard and long, and you need a little breather along the way. That's what Arianna Huffington learned the hard way, even though she's always been driven and has been working on new initiatives all her life. But she learned to do it differently. Marion visited her at the headquarters of her new company Thrive Global. It's in the middle of New York's buzzing Soho neighborhood, and the place was absolutely packed with people, workstations, food, papers, and files. Clearly the company had outgrown the space already, just 2 years after its launch. But one place was sacred: the nap room. That was always ready to welcome anybody who needed to catch up on some much needed zzz's. 'I want to change the way we live and work,' Arianna said. The former politician, writer, media person, board member, and serial entrepreneur had grown up with an outsized work ethic, which had only grown bigger as she piled on successes and responsibilities. Until she crashed. Literally. Overtired after multiple nights of hardly any sleep, she fell unconscious in her office, hitting her head against the table as she fell down. When Huffington woke up in a pool of blood, she realized that the way she lived and worked had to change. Her crash was the defining moment that inspired her to create Thrive Global, a company with a mission to help us all live a more balanced life. And Huffington became a self-proclaimed "sleep crusader", advocating that getting enough sleep is key to running the marathon of life and work. Jeff Bezos is certainly convinced of that. In his words: 'The success of my company depends on me getting 8 hours of sleep.'

The trick may actually be not to choose between the marathon and the sprint, but to reconcile them both. There will be times when you're sprinting and you're going all in. You forget about everything to prep for that important pitch. Double down to land that new customer. Submerge yourself to learn something new. By all means participate in those sprint races that also help you in your mission to have a meaningful career. And enjoy the small wins. But pick your sprint races carefully. Remember that the real race you're in is a marathon (and we're not the only ones who say that,

The trick may actually be not to choose between the marathon and the sprint, but to reconcile them both.

so does Wilfried Silon, the 80-year-old founder of one of Europe's biggest marathon clubs).

Regardless of whether you are running a marathon, a sprint race, or combining both, if you are ambitious then you are also likely to be busy and will often wonder how to prioritize between work and ... the rest of your life. Digital tools enable more of us to leave the office early to go to the gym, meet friends, or put the children to bed, and then log on from home to finish work. Or to quickly dial in for an urgent meeting while we are on holiday. You might experience the blurring lines between work and leisure as additional freedom, and see it as a sign of success to be able to balance home and work ... or you might experience this as an intrusion on your personal time. Surely, when work is never more than a swipe and click away, it's hard to ever be completely away from it. And the constant barrage of emails makes clearing your inbox like the labor of Sisyphus.

If these are the types of reflections you make, then you might, like many of us, use the traditional metaphor of a balancing scale when thinking about the combination of work and life. One side of the balance reflects work, and the other side reflects life. Feeling balanced has little to do with the amount of time we devote to life and work. Some people feel balanced even though they work 80 hours per week, others feel imbalanced with a schedule of 20 working hours. If you are out of balance, you simply need to add or remove activities on either side. Sounds simple, right? Not really. What we know for sure is that the image of a balance is actually a faulty metaphor.

It's about juggling while balancing

So if it's not a balance, then what is it? A more appropriate metaphor is probably learning to juggle while balancing. Juggling while balancing is about staying focused on what matters to you on the marathon that you're running, and not being distracted by too many other things. It is about being able to bounce from one thing to another, and to constantly shift your attention while staying focused on your environment and your long-term goals. The balls will often come at you rather randomly, and some you will catch, while some you might drop. All of that while you are balancing expectations: both your own expectations and also those of others. If that sounds discouraging to you—after all, juggling while balancing sounds pretty impossible—don't panic. The solutions may be simpler than you realize. Don't strive for perfection; even professional jugglers know that balls will eventually drop ... that's one thing they know for sure. More often than you think, others will happily pick up some of the balls if you balance your needs with theirs. And, of course, be kind when they also drop the occasional ball. After all, they are juggling while balancing as well.

Juggling while balancing is about staying focused on what matters to you.

There's more to life than you

Juggling while balancing is about reconciling the sprint races with the marathon. But it's not only about you. Different people also have different beliefs, needs, and preferences when it comes to how the boundaries between work and leisure should be managed. They are running their own sprint races and marathons as well.

It's precisely these individual differences in needs and preferences that cause tensions, misunderstandings, and feelings of imbalance, both within yourself and also in the interactions you have with colleagues, family, and friends.

What we know for sure: we all manage the boundaries between work and leisure differently

Ellen Kossek differentiates between five different styles of managing the boundaries between work and leisure.

First, there is **the integrator**, who likes their work and home life to blend. They don't mind talking to family while at the office, nor do they mind taking a work call with the sound of the grocery store in the background. They may be drafting a report from the cafeteria of the hockey club while the kids are at practice. And they would not find it at all strange to bring their kid to work once in a while.

A second style is **the separator**, who prefers to have a clear line between work and personal life. When they are at the office, they focus on work, and when they're at home, they focus on leisure. Taking a private call at work or reading an email while on vacation would make them feel hugely uncomfortable. Combining both roles makes them feel that they do neither of them justice.

Third, there are the **cyclers**, such as Chris O'Neill from Evernote, who travels non-stop but also takes regular breaks to be at home. Cyclers like to switch back and forth between the integrator and the separator, for example because they alternate between periods of business travel or seasonal peaks and calmer periods of working from home. A cycler may work tremendously hard for a few years, but then take a yearlong sabbatical to recharge, before going back to their previous work first schedule.

Finally, there are the role firsters, who prefer to either put work before anything else **(work firster)** or who prioritize life over work **(life firster)**.

Kossek, E. E. (2016). Managing Work-life Boundaries in the Digital Age. *Organizational Dynamics*, 45, 258-270.

As with all styles and preferences, you are likely to believe that your strategy is the best, and that the world would be a better place if everyone adopted your approach. And that might be the case ... in the world that you would like to live in. As a separator you might see integrators as unprofessional. Who on earth answers his/her phone while being on their bike? Well, Brent Bellm, CEO of Bigcommerce, does. Or who on earth brings a baby to work? Well, New Zealand Prime Minister Jacinda Ardern did; she made history by being the first world leader to bring a baby into the United Nations general assembly. Or, if you are an integrator, you might judge a separator for being rigid and unwilling to embrace the technological evolution. Because ... in the 21st century who on earth still refuses to open his/her laptop after 6pm? Well, during the Deepwater Horizon oil spill in 2010, the incident coordinator Peter Neffenger refused to work long hours. Not in order to have a better work–life balance, but to ensure that the crisis management approach didn't become overly dependent on him. Success sometimes means that you don't put your work first.

If there's one thing that the examples we have shared so far highlight, it is that there are multiple roads to success.

And this is exactly what Ellen Kossek's research has shown. None of these styles is better than the other. It's a matter of finding (or crafting) a style that best fits your personality. It's about managing expectations and clarifying your style. And it's about accepting other people's style and surrounding yourself with a strong support network of people, both at work and outside of work, who (most of the time) are willing to accept your style. Of course, you should not be naïve either. In many companies there is still the so-called "flexibility stigma", i.e., a stigma on people who like to work flexibly. Flexibility is often something you need to earn over time. And if you work for a company full of work firsters, and you are the only life firster ... then you might not become the company's next CEO. What we know for sure is that your performance will have a big impact on how others perceive your commitment to work. If you're good at what you do, people will give you a pass to deviate from the norms every now and then.

Also, no matter what your style is, work has a sneaky habit of taking over your life. You may be a reluctant integrator, not because you chose that style but because you don't know how to manage any other way. Or you may suffer from "job creep", as work seems to infiltrate in all corners of your life. To avoid this from happening, Michelle Obama applied a very simple trick: she formally scheduled non-work commitments on Barack Obama's formal agenda (such as going to the dentist, attending the kids' music recital, etc.). So if you want to make sure that work

It's about managing expectations and clarifying your style. And it's about accepting other people's style.

doesn't take over your hobbies, sports, or family time, make sure that you also schedule your non-work commitments. If Barack and Michelle Obama can do it, so can you!

Finally, realize that your life outside of work doesn't need to distract you from having a successful professional life. Your leisure time can actually teach you important work skills. We admit, changing diapers or bargaining with a teenager about screen time doesn't sound very alluring, but they do teach us skills such as multitasking and negotiating.

What we know for sure: happiness at work goes hand in hand with happiness at home

If you're fully engaged in work, does that mean there is no room for anything else? The reverse is actually true. A 2016 study surveyed 746 employees of 12 different organizations. The goal was to find out whether or not work engagement has an enriching effect on other areas of life. Being engaged with your work means that you throw your full energy into it: physical, emotional, and cognitive. In other words, you make full use of your body, your heart, and your brain at work.

As the results show, people who do that are actually happier with their life overall. This is what we call "the work-home spillover effect". And they are also more involved in other activities in their community. So it doesn't appear that the rest of your life necessarily needs to suffer because you are fully engaged with your work. Happiness at work actually goes hand in hand with happiness in life!

Eldor, L., I. Harpaz and M. Westman. (2016). The Work/Nonwork Spillover: The Enrichment Role of Work Engagement. *Journal of Leadership & Organizational Studies*, May 2016.

Take it from us

What do we wish that we had known? Well, that viewing life as marathon, and not as a combination of sprint races, surely helps a lot. That a well-selected sprint race every now and then does not hurt and will not knock you off the right track. That juggling while balancing is plain fun, as long as you accept that balls will get dropped.

And what do we know for sure? That balance is bogus. Maybe we should just forget about the whole notion of work-life balance. After all, who ever said you're not fully living when you're working? It's not like you pause your life when you're at work. How sad is it if you can't embrace the social contacts, the learning experiences, and the fulfillment that work can bring you, as if that is not part of life. What you should look for is harmony between the different parts of your life, and the different roles you have. And be content with your own choices on how to balance it all.

Go for the growth mindset.

6 Make learning your job

The myth: learning stops at graduation

I have no special talent, I'm only passionately curious.

Albert Einstein

"Earn a degree and get a job". You probably heard this quite a few times while growing up. And you won't hear us arguing anything else, what did you expect? But in a world that is constantly evolving and is flooded by highly educated talent, the mere fact of having a degree is not a guarantee of professional accomplishment ... no, not even a degree from a world-class business school in Belgium that starts with a V. The fact is, graduation is an illusion. Because you will never really be done with learning.

We don't want to dismiss all the blood, sweat, and tears you shed in the process of earning your degree... But let's admit it: as long as you are going to school, learning is pretty straightforward. You simply have to learn what the teachers tell you to learn in order to become the person you want to be "when you grow up". And you probably questioned those same teachers for exposing you to all that "useless stuff", secretly quoting Pink Floyd's "We don't need no education". But what you didn't admit was that it was also pretty comfortable having others telling you what to learn. The more you "grow up", the less you will experience such comfort and the more you will need to take charge of your own learning. And that can be quite daunting. Of all the countless things you could be learning, what skills should you be investing in? How can you ensure that you're future-proof? What if ten years from now you find out that you took a "wrong" turn and your skills have become outdated?

Don't worry. That's a problem that many people before you have faced. It's also the story of the movie "Hidden Figures" (based on the book with the same title by Margot Lee Shetterly). The movie tells the real story of 3 brilliant women. Working for NASA in the early 60s, they are human computers: mathematicians who work on making manned space travel possible. One of them, Dorothy, finds out about plans to install an IBM 7090 electronic computer. It's clear to her that her job, and those of her fellow "human computers", will be at risk once the machine takes over. She faces the exact challenge that Silicon Valley entrepreneur Marc Andreessen would describe 50 years later as 'The spread of computers and the internet will put people in two categories: those who tell computers what to do and those who are told by computers what to do.' Dorothy goes to the library to find out more, and starts studying. After teaching herself programming she is promoted to lead the programming department (and become the first African-American supervisor at NASA).

If there is one thing we know for sure, it is that ten years from now you will indeed find out that many of your skills will have become outdated, and that the only way to make yourself future-proof is to keep on learning, again and again. In the words of Arie de Geus, a business theorist, 'The ability to learn faster than your competitors may be your only sustainable competitive advantage.' Because you can only continue to lead if you continue to learn. That may sound like plain common sense to you. But what we also know for sure is that the more experience we gain, the more we resist doing entirely new things and the more biased we become against pushing ourselves to acquire radically new capabilities. Such learning requires a true openness to being that "rookie" over and over again.

If there is one thing we know for sure, it is that ten years from now you will indeed find out that many of your skills will have become outdated. What we also know for sure is that the more experience we gain, the more we resist doing entirely new things.

Zen Buddhism has a word for this state of mind: they call it "Shoshin", or a beginner's mind. It means having an attitude that is open and without preconceptions, just as a beginner would. Even when you're already very good at something, you can still keep a beginner's mind. The sense of wonder that comes with it makes you constantly look at the world with a fresh pair of eyes. This is because the more you know, the more you know you don't know (here's Aristotle again). In the first email he sent as the new CEO of Microsoft, Satya Nadella reminded all employees: 'I fundamentally believe that if you are not learning new things, you stop doing great and useful things' ... 'I buy more books than I can finish. I sign up for more online courses than I can complete.' Your appetite for learning is also what will get you hired. At Google, the one defining trait that they are looking for is the natural drive to learn. What the company needs, according to CEO Eric Schmidt, is "learning animals."

How to spot the learning animal

The learning spirit is not so much about the amount of certificates and degrees you collect. What matters is your fundamental attitude. It has nothing to do with classrooms and college campuses. Being a learning animal is about being curious, humble, and brave.

Harry Truman once said: 'Not all readers are leaders, but all leaders are readers.' Lifelong learning starts with lifelong curiosity. Be careful to give your curiosity a purpose. This is not the same thing as the curiosity that makes you scroll endlessly through your Instagram feed. You probably know the feeling that your information consumption is dictated by your social media feeds, which propel you from one subject to another like a ball in a pinball machine. Ironically, we have never had more access to information, which makes it ever harder to focus and learn something. There's so much available that we constantly collect information without really absorbing it. Make sure that you put a filter on every once in a while. Read a book from start to finish. Take the time to go deep into a subject, without distractions. Roch Doliveux, former CEO of UCB, put it like this: 'Every year I ask myself what I want to learn this year. And then I really dive in deeply. You need to be willing to learn something in depth. I once spent 3 full days learning how to do hiring interviews. I'm sure you can read one article about it and feel you know what it takes. But you will not really remember the lessons and for sure will not be able to put them into practice.'

Harry Truman once said: 'Not all readers are leaders, but all leaders are readers.'

Learning animals are also fundamentally humble. They know there is something to learn in every situation. As Socrates said: 'Stupid people already have all the answers, smart people learn from everything and everyone.' Being humble means that you know it's always possible to create a better version of yourself, and that you are never finished. Being lucky enough to have received higher education is actually a trap. This is because the more we're educated and the more experience we gain, the more we think we can resolve anything based on experience and instinct. And that's a dangerous hypothesis in fast-changing times. So make sure your speed of learning is faster than the speed in which the world around you changes!

Make sure your speed of learning is faster than the speed in which the world around you changes!

Finally, learning animals are brave. The truth is, learning happens somewhere between your comfort zone and your panic zone. Preferably not too close to your panic zone, but clearly beyond your comfort zone. Learning requires effort, and it is uncomfortable. If you don't feel in the slightest bit uncomfortable, it's a sign that you are not actually learning. Let's face it, once you have finished school, you're relieved not to have to pass any more tests. Even the tests you put yourself through. Doing something you've never done before, or immersing yourself in a domain that you're not familiar with, is not exactly the easiest road to take. Being a learning animal means you're actively seeking that discomfort, until eventually you can't really exist without it, as life is pretty boring if you don't.

What we know for sure: being a high performer does not make you a good learner

People that you would assume to be great learners are often not. Chris Argyris discovered this by studying management consultants. He assumed they would be great examples of good learners, as they are typically highly educated and smart (and many of them have got where they are because of their learning abilities) and it's their job to help other organizations and managers improve. He found the opposite. Instead of finding examples of effective learning, he found that they were great at firefighting and problem-solving, but that they found it very difficult to reflect critically on their own performance. Having been successful for most their lives, they had had very little practice in the introspection that is needed to diagnose one's own shortcomings and failures, which is needed if you are to correct them next time.

High performers also have a more difficult time than other people when they are learning, because they are simply not used to the inevitable feeling of being a failure that comes with learning. In order to avoid that uncomfortable feeling, they consistently look for something or someone else to blame when something does not go as well as it should, instead of reflecting on what they could do better or differently themselves.

Argyris, C. (1991). Teaching Smart People How to Learn. *Harvard Business Review*, May-June 1991.

Fly on the wings of your strengths (but don't think you are stuck with your weaknesses)

Now, the bigger question you might be asking yourself is whether it is better to invest in further developing and refining your strengths, or whether you should go for the tough track and overcome your weaknesses? In other words, if you're not a numbers person, should you invest in becoming one? Or would you be better off focusing your energy on refining your already well-developed language skills? Most of us prefer the latter. Unsurprisingly, it feels so much better to further develop what you're already good at than to face the brutal confrontation with your shortcomings. Even subconsciously, you may find yourself seeking out those challenges where your strengths will shine and your weaknesses can be swept under the rug. But that's a dangerous trap, and it's called the competency trap. We fall into a competency trap when we keep doing more of the things that we do well, because we enjoy doing them. Ultimately, we become so excellent in those skills that we just don't want to let go of all the hard work that led us to achieve excellence in the first place. But by overinvesting in our strengths, we also take less time to learn other important new skills. This is because it feels more costly to go back to the status of being a rookie in an entirely new field. Once you're in the competency trap, the mere thought of being a novice again and being dumb, awkward, and slow becomes extremely scary. Now, we're not saying that you shouldn't play to your strengths. What we are saying is that many people already have a tendency to use their strengths as an excuse not to develop their weaknesses. So if you're the creative one, challenge yourself on the quantitative side. If you're the Excel wizard, don't automatically assume that role in a team. If you're scared of standing in front of an audience, take every opportunity to practice your presentation skills. You may actually surprise yourself. What you thought was a weakness, may turn out to become your strength.

Remember how your first olive tasted? Disgusting, right? But over time, many of us have learned to appreciate them. One of Katleen's friends, Pieter, is an enthusiast of what she would call "dissonant" music. He can inform you in detail about the subtle ingenuity of artists like Captain Beefheart and Sonic Youth, while to her the music just sounds like a whole lot of noise. But over time she has learnt to appreciate (some) of the music he has recommended to her. Just like olives and dissonant music, the tasks that we despise and avoid the most because we're bad at them can become an acquired taste. But why on earth would you embark on acquiring a new taste when your own taste is there, without any effort? The answer is that acquired tastes are so much more rewarding and allow you to grow in your capacity to enjoy what the world has to offer.

What we know for sure: a growth mindset propels you further

Luckily there are some research-based remedies that help to fight against the competency trap. The most powerful remedy is probably to embrace what Caroll Dweck would call a "growth mindset". Caroll Dweck's influential work shows that people tend to hold one of two mindsets when it comes to learning and the malleability of their capabilities: a fixed or a growth mindset. A fixed mindset reflects a belief that human qualities (e.g. intelligence, character, and skills) are largely fixed and very hard to develop/change. A growth mindset reflects a belief that human qualities can be developed through effort, persistence, and learning. These seemingly small beliefs have been found to profoundly impact the extent to which we are truly willing to invest in the development of entirely new capabilities and to embrace the challenges and setbacks that come with learning. Interestingly, you can lead a successful life if you have either a fixed or a growth mindset. At least, if you are one of the happy few who never faces a setback, or who never has to deal with change. It's in turbulent times that your mindset will become a true differentiator. And in today's world, turbulence is the norm. So let's have a closer look at how your mindset impacts how you deal with change and setbacks.

The research undertaken by Caroll Dweck and her colleagues shows that those who embrace a growth mindset see challenges and obstacles as an opportunity to develop themselves. As a consequence, they are more likely to take a calculated leap into the unknown and to experiment with new and innovative approaches ... not only once, but constantly. They recognize that success isn't simply handed to them on a plate, but that it is important to persist, even after a setback.

In contrast, those with a fixed mindset believe that talents should feel "natural" and that talent determines how quickly you can pick up a skill. When they are confronted with a setback, they become filled with self-doubt and tend to see this as a lack of talent on their part. As a result, they may give up and not work hard to overcome the obstacle ... after all, when you are talented, everything should go smoothly. As a consequence, they tend to overinvest in their positive qualities and avoid confronting their problems so that they don't make a fool of themselves, and they tend to worry about being criticized. So the crucial question is: is your mindset fixed or can you change your mindset? Fortunately, you can learn to embrace a growth mindset. In fact, most people actually have a mixed mindset. They believe that certain skills (e.g. financial skills) can be developed, but that others (e.g. empathy) can't. So how can you learn to embrace a growth mindset? By surrounding yourself with people who naturally have a growth mindset. But, first of all, take notice of your self-talk and pay attention to the micro-messages you give to others. Well-intended messages, such as 'You're a natural' or 'Look at how quickly you learned that', inadvertently stimulate a fixed mindset, while growth-minded messages recognize efforts, for example 'Look at how quickly you picked that up, you must have had a great learning strategy' or 'Look at how authentic your presentation looked, it's clear you put a lot of effort into it'.

Dweck, C. (2007). *Mindset: the new psychology of success.* Ballantine Books.

Katleen remembers: 'I certainly didn't always have a growth mindset, I had a mixed mindset at best. I was convinced that hard work would get me my degree and assure me of an income, but beyond that, I felt that it was all about the talent. After all, everyone is hard-working, no? So it's only talent that differentiates good from great. In retrospect, I could not have been more wrong. But this false belief filled me with lots of self-doubts when embarking on my PhD journey. In the back of my head was this constant question: am I really capable of this? What if they find out that I'm not as talented as they think I am? I even had this mindset in other areas in life: I simply did not have the DNA to be any good at sports, and I was hopeless at drawing because of a lack of talent. Luckily I had other talents to conceal my shortcomings. Then something changed. During my PhD journey, I got the opportunity to spend a year in the US, where I worked with Sue Ashford, a top professor in my field. Meeting the superwoman behind all those papers I had been reading made me nervous and I couldn't understand why she agreed to it in the first place. In my mind, she was a true "natural" ... at least, until I met her! When I saw first-hand how much thought and effort she was putting into her work, I understood that she wasn't this larger-than-life person that I imagined her to be. She was just a very hard-working woman who was very disciplined and thoughtful about what she did ... and she was working out in the gym as well! And that made me respect her even more ... I started to feel that I could potentially accomplish some of these things as well, which was a transformational moment for me. That same year, I published my own research in a journal that I thought was completely out of my reach ... I even ran my first 10K that year and more recently also my first marathon (my high school gym teacher probably still can't believe that I have become a runner). Embracing a growth mindset has transformed me completely.'

Take it from us

The ability to acquire new skills and knowledge quickly and continually is crucial to success in a world of rapid change. In that sense, we're all condemned to lifelong learning. So why not enjoy the process and embark on the exciting journey of developing a growth mindset? Perhaps we should all think a bit more like Felix Van de Maele, co-founder and CEO of Collibra, who says that one of his personal keys to staying flexible in his CEO role in a continuously growing and changing company is to embrace a growth mindset and accept that there are many areas in which he needs to grow. It's really like our opening quote of Albert Einstein says: 'I have no special talents, I'm only passionately curious.'

How do you shine while still being uniquely you?

7 Become your best self

The myth: you should fake it till you make it

Be yourself. Everyone else is already taken.

Oscar Wilde

The candidate in front of us looked nervous. His sweaty palms when he shook our hands had revealed that. You could see red blotches of skin next to his shirt collar. It was all understandable. You don't do an admissions interview to get into business school every day, and it is a stressful occasion, even for the most cool-headed among us. The next 20 minutes could literally change the direction of his life. For us, at the other side of the table, it was a lot more comfortable. All four of us had done literally hundreds of admissions interviews as part of the jury. We had just gone over this candidate's application file and were quite intrigued. He was not the typical candidate. He had done none of the usual internships and student jobs and he had no economic background whatsoever. But he had studied pharmaceutical sciences and obtained good grades. He was captain of his soccer team and had worked a factory job every summer. Could this be the diamond in the rough we so loved to discover? We kicked it off with an easy warm-up question. 'What do you see yourself doing after your master's program?' It's hard to give a wrong answer to this question.

Just about any answer could be right, and could be used by the candidate to show their drive, talent, or uniqueness and spin it in their favor. Not this time. 'So I really want to work for a big pharmaceutical company as a manager.' 'Cool, so could you give us an example of what company that could be? Just, like, name a name?' ... Silence ensued ... nothing. Except more red blotches. And in the end he just stammered 'I don't really know any companies.'

When you want to make a good first impression, it can be tempting to not entirely be yourself. We have seen it so often. People say what they think you want to hear. But they fall through the cracks at the slightest probing. Have you fallen into this trap before? Particularly when you want to make a good first impression, you may desperately try to say and do the right thing. And if you're a people pleaser, it may have become second nature to guess what other people expect from you and try to deliver it.

The candidate did not pass the interview. After the first question he had completely blanked and his nerves had gotten the better of him. When asked later on why he had said he wanted to work for a big pharmaceutical company when he did not even know any, he confessed 'I just thought that's what you wanted to hear. In reality I've come to the conclusion that doing pharmaceutical sciences was a wrong choice, and I want to make a 180 degree turn to something completely different. I just don't know what that would be yet, and hoped to discover it here.'

Shooting from the hip in the name of authenticity is not very considerate.

Saying what you think people want to hear is almost never a good idea. It makes you nervous, and that is never a good look. And you can never keep up the charade. So you don't want to be a phony who is full of baloney. But let's face it. We all need to fake it a little bit to make it. Surely you wouldn't do a job interview and confess to the fact that you had to google some of the stuff they put in the job profile? But you can also be "too authentic". Shooting from the hip in the name of authenticity is not very considerate. 'I'm just being myself' becomes an excuse for just not caring about your impact on others. It's like that friend who's always late, and doesn't even make an effort any more to come up with an excuse. "I'm just really bad at leaving on time." Being authentic is not an excuse to let it all hang out!

So how can you manage this odd tension between being inauthentic and being too authentic? And more importantly, how do you shine while still being uniquely you? Let's get real!

Who are you really?

Being authentic is about being true to yourself. And that's a necessary ingredient of happiness. It's like Paul Bulcke, the chairman of Nestlé, says: 'Authenticity may be a buzzword now, but it's actually extremely important. You can never be happy if you're not yourself. Of course you can work on the packaging, but the content should always be you.'

However, it requires a large amount of self-knowledge to know who you are. Most of us spend our entire life discovering our true self and we never really complete the process. Life is an eternal process of self-discovery, if only because you have so many different dimensions, and you're also constantly changing. Think of the different facets of who you are in terms of the different friends you have. You may have one friend you always go running with. A bunch of friends you only meet for after-work drinks on Thursday evening. The couple of friends you can always rely on to discover the latest and hippest new restaurant or bar. There are the other parents from school that you chat with while arranging the carpool. The work friend you have lunch with to discuss the latest office gossip. Are you yourself with each of these friends? Sure you are. But they know different parts of you and connect to the different roles you have, in which different dimensions of your personality come to the forefront.

Being true to yourself still leaves a lot of space for the different versions of you to manifest themselves. You have more than one true self. So don't restrict yourself to a limited self-concept. Not only does it rob you of the opportunity to explore different layers of your identity, it also limits your learning. In the words of leadership guru Herminia Ibarra: 'A very simple definition of authenticity is being true to self. But self could be who I am today, who I've always been or who I might be tomorrow.' Authenticity contains the risk of limiting your growth. As you're thinking "Well, that's simply not me", you can safely stay within your comfort zone. You may have suffered from more than one college professor who clung to their identity as a hard-core researcher, so they did not need to also develop into a good teacher. By wrapping themselves in the safety blanket of their researcher identity, they prevented their teacher identity from blossoming. To learn something new means that you need to make yourself comfortable with new ideas and behaviors. In the beginning, that will always

Being true to yourself still leaves a lot of space for the different versions of you.

feel a bit unnatural and fake. For example, if you learn a new language, you will not feel at all authentic as you utter your first hesitant sentences and try to have a "spontaneous" conversation. Marion relates: 'When I first moved to the US, I spoke decent English. Decent enough to have conversations and even give presentations. But not decent enough to make an impromptu joke or make a quick-witted reply to a comment, as I could do in my native language. Being a non-native speaker among born-and-raised Americans, I felt entirely robbed of my personality and like I truly could not be my authentic self. It took me several months to make that level of language mastery my own, so that I could show others the real me.'

The real you—as seen by others

Wanting to manage other people's perceptions of you is very human–it would even be disrespectful not to do so. People all over the world spend billions on clothes, cosmetics, and hairdressers–all intended to make them more attractive to others. Impression management plays an important role in our own well-being and that of others. Let's admit it, your Instagram account is entirely an effort in impression management.

A true master of combining impression management and authenticity is Chiara Ferragni. The Italian digital phenomenon and uber-influencer has a whopping 20 million followers on Instagram. Her feed and constant stream of stories are a perfect blend of aspirational pictures (Chiara in lingerie, Chiara with a closet full of Hermes bags, Chiara with her superstar husband in seductive poses) and completely relatable content (Chiara making lasagna, Chiara playing with her 2-year-old boy, Chiara being goofy on TikTok and showing her completely clumsy dancing skills, etc.). Meanwhile, the tracksuits and tank tops from her clothing brand sell like hotcakes, and she is raking in millions in brand deals.

Being authentic does not only help you, it also very much influences the way you relate to others and the impact you have on them. Who do you want to be friends with? Who do you want to work with? Who do you want to be led by? People who you believe to be real, honest, and sincere. So being a friend, colleague, or leader requires authenticity. That's why great leaders work hard on actively managing their authenticity. Because they realize that being seen as authentic is absolutely essential in order for people to want to follow you. It's something that Steve Jobs did masterfully. Even through his dress code. His trademark sneakers, dad-jeans, and black turtleneck signaled very clearly 'Trust me, I am myself in every situation, because I look the same in every situation. What you see is what you get.' Contrast this with the way Mark Zuckerberg looked as he was interrogated by the American congress on the way Facebook dealt with private data. He had tossed his signature look of jeans and a gray t-shirt for the occasion and dressed up in a suit and tie. The *New York Times* called it the "I'm sorry" suit. But the sorry was not entirely convincing. This was because Mark Zuckerberg looked like a dressed up schoolboy: uncomfortable and phony. Robotically answering questions, he came across as anything but authentic.

You don't decide all by yourself whether or not you are authentic. Telling others that you're authentic would be like telling people that you have good taste. If you have to tell them ... you probably haven't. Authenticity is defined by what other people see in you. But just like with acting, there is a very thin line between showing the best version of yourself and just plain lying.

You don't decide all by yourself whether or not you are authentic.

Establishing your authenticity requires two things. Firstly, if you want people to perceive you as authentic then you need to ensure that your words match your actions. And secondly, you need people to relate to you by finding common ground. And this means that sometimes you will indeed need to present different faces to different audiences. And that's the part that many of us find hard to reconcile with authenticity. Shakespeare recognized this long ago: 'All the world's a stage ... and one man in his time plays many parts.' And such role playing doesn't have to be insincere. Imagine that, after reading this book, you decide to pursue an MBA. It's very likely that you will convey this message very differently to your parents than to your kids, and differently again to your current employer. Your message will be the same, but the way you deliver it will be very different.

What acting can teach us about authenticity

This may come as a surprise to you, but we can learn a lot from actors about what it takes to be real. Unquestionably, actors put on a mask to convince us that they are someone else. But the greatest actors of all realize that acting is not about being someone different. They bring themselves and their own life experiences into the roles they play in order to create their characters. To put it in Johnny Depp's words: 'With any part you play, there's a big amount of yourself in it. There has to be, otherwise it's just not acting. It would be lying.' And that's exactly how authenticity works.

Psychologist Mark Snyder from the University of Minnesota identified two psychological profiles that inform us about authenticity. On the one hand, there are the "high self-monitors", who care about their public image, adapt to the demands of a situation, and sometimes even wear a mask without feeling fake. They are true chameleons who are capable of adapting to the demands of their environment, yet they do not lose their identities in the process. On the other hand, there are the "low self-monitors", who prefer to be true to themselves and express indiscriminately what they really think and feel. Interestingly, the people that we label as being authentic are often not the low self-monitors but the true chameleons: those people who know exactly which of their personality traits they should reveal to whom and when. They basically do what great actors or chameleons do; they stay true to who they are, but they know quite naturally when to show which version of themselves.

What we know for sure: faking it makes you nervous

A typical situation in which you have a first meeting and want to make a good impression is when an entrepreneur pitches for potential investors. In doing their pitch, entrepreneurs may want to cater to what investors want to hear. Another such situation is doing a job interview. You really want the job, so you're willing to say whatever is needed to get it. A typical tactic used in these situations is called catering. It's a form of impression management that is not really meant to show off or make you look perfect but is oriented toward the person you want to impress. You see a miniature car in the office of the senior manager you're meeting, and you suddenly fake an interest in cars. There's a picture of him shaking hands with a famous soccer player, and you suddenly find yourself using soccer metaphors in your pitch. Or you read that the investor you're pitching to is a people person, so suddenly you're stressing what a team player you are.

But this type of catering to others doesn't do you any favors. The reason for this is not that you fail to fool the other person. It's more that you fail to fool yourself. And that makes you nervous. And it's the nerves that make you stumble. A few nerves, of course, don't do any harm. Research in law courts has even shown that when lawyers express a little uncertainty or doubt in their communication, and even stumble over their words, this actually signals that they recognize that they don't know everything and don't want to take control entirely.

Gino, F., O. Sezer, L. Huang. (2020). To be or not to be your Authentic Self? Catering to Others' Preferences Hinders Performance. *Organizational Behavior and Human Decision Processes*, in press.

There is the you that procrastinates until the very end before a deadline. There is the you that is able to improvise and make a killer presentation, even after working an all-nighter to make that deadline. Let's face it, you have your best assets. And you also have some, let's put it diplomatically, areas of improvement. But let's forget about these for a minute and only focus on the good. Most of us develop some sense of who we are when we are at our best. Stored deep down inside, we all have some idea of the traits we bring to the table when we really shine.

However, getting a good sense of that best self is not always easy. That's because we're all biased toward the negative comments. Most people are pretty bad at receiving compliments. We quickly brush them off: 'Really, that was a good presentation? I was really just winging it. I'm just lucky nobody noticed.' Contrary to this, we have an elephant's memory for negative feedback. (Confession by Marion: 'I still remember my grandma commenting I was getting a bit chubby. 35 years ago!') When you receive 9 positive comments and 1 negative comment, it's undoubtedly the negative one that you dwell on and which keeps lingering in your mind.

We also tend to believe that giving and receiving feedback is about pinpointing what can be improved. And, of course, that's useful. But it's learning about your strengths and about those moments when you are at your best that allows you to construct an image of what your best self looks like. So, when something goes really well for you, play back the tape in your mind. And try to understand exactly what you did that made it a success and what traits you leveraged. Notice when you get positive feedback. And also ask for it! Yes, that sounds vain and like fishing for compliments. But when you frame it as a sincere interest in understanding what you bring to the table and how you can make an even better contribution, you can do it. Over time, you'll develop a more nuanced and detailed picture of your best self. It's like painting your most flattering self-portrait.

Notice when you get positive feedback. And also ask for it!

The beauty is, this self-portrait isn't some rosy-colored product of your imagination. It's you entirely. In fact, other people may see it better than you do (maybe because other people aren't there when you spend an entire Sunday in your pajamas, binge-watching Netflix, and eating that entire pint of Ben & Jerry's). This could also be because you may be blind to those days when you bring your A-game. Successful people are attuned to what that A-game is. So they can be authentic and kill it at the same time. The better you understand it, the more you can craft it, polish it, and bring it out more frequently and with better effect. Don't be shy in asking for the help you need in doing the crafting and polishing work. Even the most successful and established people do. Like Eric Schmidt, former CEO of Google, who admitted in an interview with Fortune: 'The one thing people are never good at, is seeing themselves as others see them. A coach can really help.' To be your best natural self, sometimes mother nature just needs a helping hand.

What we know for sure: how you paint your best self-portrait

Your reflected best self is your individual mental picture of the qualities and characteristics that are on display when you are at your best. But how do you construct this mental picture? Typically, it's by getting glimpses in a rare and imperfect mirror that reflects back your best self. We then construct a patchwork quilt of imperfect and incomplete reflections, composed mostly on the fly. So it's useful to understand how you can get a sharper image and how you can paint a more detailed self-portrait. What are the trigger events that contain new pieces of information to add to the picture?

There are 4 types of these trigger events. They can be either formal or informal. And they can either be challenging you or appreciative. A formal and challenging trigger event is, for example, when you get a new assignment at work that really stretches you, and you pull it off. An informal and challenging trigger event can be when you are thrown into the deep end and discover that you can actually swim. For example, when you have an important appointment with a client and your more senior colleague unexpectedly calls in sick. A formal but appreciative trigger event is when you receive official accolades. You may win an award, for example, or be called "colleague of the month" for something you did. And finally, the last type of trigger event is informal and appreciative. It's the spontaneous compliment you get that catches you by surprise. Next time that happens to you, don't brush it off, but actually pause and think about it.

Morgan Roberts, L., J. Dutton, G. Spreitzer, E. Heaphy, R. Quinn. (2005). Composing the Reflected Best-Self Portrait: Building Pathways for Becoming Extraordinary in Work Organizations. *Academy of Management Review,* 30 (4), 712-736.

Morgan Roberts L., E. D. Heaphy, B. Barker Caza. (2019). To Become your Best Self, Study your Successes. *Harvard Business Review,* 14 May 2019.

Take it from us

Very often you'll find that people are mild copies of each other ... because we all like to "belong". Our need to belong may drive us to conformity. And while conformity feels safe, it also makes things boring and uninspiring. Dare to be yourself, and you will always be "original". Dare to be you, in all your glory—your strengths and skills, as well as your flaws and insecurities. No one can do a better you than you. But also realize that there are many versions of you and that "you" are in constant evolution. Probably the best version of yourself is the one that is constantly looking for a better version of yourself. And that's for real.

Can anyone really be self-made?

8 Seek out the tough love

The myth: a good boss/ mentor is understanding and supportive

It's high time you were shown that you really don't know all there is to be known.

Dr. Seuss

You did it! "It" could refer to anything you have accomplished: getting your degree, being promoted, or launching a business. Whatever "it" is that you have accomplished, it's likely that you will find one constant: it is "you" who did "it". Good for you! But can anyone really be self-made? We all want to believe that we achieve success in both our life and our career by ourselves, that we are the sole architects of our success. But actually, we are suffering from the fundamental attribution error: taking credit for our successes, without acknowledging the impact of others (and, even worse, blaming our failures on those same people as well).

The reality is that the people close to you have a huge impact on your accomplishments. Behind every success are significant investments and sacrifices by some (if not all!) of the following people: family, friends, fans, opponents, advisors, teachers, writers, mentors, and so on. Often it is our pride, ego, insecurity, or ignorance that keeps us from recognizing the contributions of these people.

Some of these are people you cannot choose for yourself. For better or for worse, your parents are who they are. And, like you, they are far from perfect. If they berated you for not making your bed, they may have traumatized you for life ... or they might actually have been doing you a favor, who can tell? As Rafiki, the mandrill in the "Lion King" would say: 'The past can hurt. You can either run from it or learn from it.' Sometimes you just hit the jackpot, and somebody comes onto your path and you're incredibly lucky to have met them at the right time and place.

The search for applause

You may tend to believe that it is your boss who selected you. After all, applying for a job feels like a professional beauty contest, in which you are vetted from all sides and, if all goes well, you're crowned the winner at the end. But what if you look at it from the other side? What if you could choose your boss instead of the other way around? Let's face it, in today's war for talent it is often the employer who enters the beauty contest. What would be your selection criteria? What kind of person do you want to report to? If your answer to this question is someone who encourages and endorses me, and who appreciates and recognizes my hard work, you are not alone. Most people want to get lots of positive feedback and encouragement. We say we want feedback, but actually we want applause. In the same way that we are addicted to social media likes, we want to amass real life likes as well. And it's very human to seek approval and want to be validated. We all want to feel good, and what feels better than to be nurtured and complimented?

But actually we're wrong. It's not in a soft climate that we flourish the most. Think back to those moments in your life when you learned the most valuable lessons. Did that happen as a consequence of a resounding victory? Did you learn the most from those things you succeeded at easily? Or was it the tough times that taught you the most? Let's face it, we often make the most progress with the right combination of encouragement and challenge. Every karate kid needs a Mr. Miyagi, right?

Marion recalls: 'I remember being a doctoral student at Wharton. In preparing to go on the job market, I and my fellow doctoral students got the opportunity to present our work to the senior faculty of the department. When it was my turn, I was nervous and excited. I had carefully prepared a slide deck, rehearsed it through and through, thought through all possible questions and comments that I could come up with and felt I was as ready as I could ever be. But I was not entirely prepared for what unfolded. In my 1-hour allotted time slot, I only got to slide 7, not even close to being halfway through. The professors around the table kept throwing questions at me. They questioned just about every single word I said. Tricked me into contradicting myself. Started whole discussions amongst themselves. It was horrible and after about one hour, I was relieved to get out alive.

I was convinced that I should give up my ambition to secure a professor position at a top American university. I did not sleep at all that night and dragged my feet the next day as I did not want to go back to campus and be confronted with the same people who had torn me to shreds the day before. When I heard that my peers had a similar experience I was a bit consoled. I decided I had nothing to lose, and that I would go on anyway. At worst, I would expand my network and learn from the process. At best I would succeed, although the chance of that happening seemed pretty slim to me now. What I did not know at the time was that I had passed a crucial hurdle. Those same people that challenged me started giving valuable advice. They spent time coaching me and my peers and shared their own experiences. Some of them spontaneously offered to write me a recommendation letter. Over the next few months I got the opportunity to interview with quite a few big name universities. And while the thought of that would have been terrifying to me before, the worst was actually behind me. It was all relatively easy and friendly, after that first disastrous dry-run. In truth, my work had improved a lot as a result.

Looking back now, I am incredibly grateful. The fact that some of the most renowned and talented people in the field took the time to listen to my research was an incredible opportunity. They taught me what kind of critique I would need to be able to deal with at the highest level. Yes, they were tough, but they were tough because they wanted to help me succeed and they knew the bar was set high.'

All mentors have a way of seeing more of our faults than we would like. It's the only way we grow (yes, Star Wars is right). Does that mean that you should seek mentors who undermine you whenever they get the chance? Of course not. "Tough" managers often mistakenly think that it is safer to be firm and a little bit distant. But what research actually shows is that this only increases stress. Adam Grant shows that nice guys and ladies are actually more effective because they create trust. But the greatest mentors of all possess the right mix of encouragement and challenge. They know when to be soft and they know when to be tough, and they use both approaches in the right doses.

The greatest mentors of all possess the right mix of encouragement and challenge.

Push without breaking

So how do you recognize a great supervisor or mentor? It's not by how much attention and praise they give you. It's by their ability to push you forward, and to know exactly how much to push without breaking you. This is something that sportspeople and their coaches know all too well. Marc Lammers coached the Dutch ladies team to Olympic gold in field hockey in 2008. To get there, he needed to get the best out of his team, and bring them to their best possible performance. In an effort to get his ladies to their maximum physical fitness, he introduced a technique he picked up from horse racing. To make the horses recover quickly from an exhausting race, they are put into a bath of ice water. So Marc thought that if it works for horses, why not for humans? One day after daily training he brought in a whole bunch of ice baths for each of the girls to go into. The girls thought he was crazy. Surely he wouldn't expect them to actually do this? One brave one tried and lasted all of 30 seconds in the freezing water. But Marc persisted. He told them that if they really wanted to win Olympic gold then they needed to go further than their competitors. It's not by doing conventional things they would get exceptional results. Reluctantly the girls got into the freezing bathtubs, encouraging each other to stay in as long as was bearable. From then on, this became standard practice after every training session.

What we know for sure: tough love leads to results

Research has investigated whether a "softer" culture or a "harder" culture leads to better results. A soft culture is characterized by things like decision-making by consensus and a warm organizational climate. A hard culture is associated with individual accountability, strong direction-setting, and an acceptance of conflict. Both can be effective in certain situations, but what we call "tough love" cultures work best. You can recognize them by their very strong shared performance-driven values, where feedback is given frequently and immediately.

A tough love culture requires leaders to have a broad behavioral repertoire and the ability to perform roles that include a degree of contradiction or paradox. They can shift between either a hard or soft approach, and they know when to use each of those approaches. They are able to reach out to people and give them unconditional support, while also demanding that they be the best they can be.

The kind of nurturing and warmth that is present in a tough love environment creates a context where people are willing to accept (and gain the benefits of) being pressured to go beyond what they would ordinarily do. Think of your personal trainer getting you to do just one more set of sit-ups than you would do when training by yourself.

> Kelman, S. and S. Hong. (2012). Hard, Soft, or Tough Love: What Kinds of Organizational Culture Promote Successful Performance in Cross-Organizational Collaborations? *HKS Faculty Research Working Paper Series RWP12-005*, John F. Kennedy School of Government, Harvard University.

So what should you look for in a great mentor or sponsor? The best bosses are actually not the sweetest. They are the ones that care enough to take the trouble to tell you when you are going too far or just not far enough.

Marion recounts: 'I vividly remember one evening when I was in the third year of Engineering school. I had come home to my parents' house, in a grumpy and self-pitying mood. My life was tough, so I felt. Too much studying, too much work, too many tests. When my dad came home, I jumped on the opportunity to offload on him, hoping that he would commiserate with me. The exact opposite happened. I wasn't even halfway through my complaints when he stopped me and told me in plain and simple terms that I had to snap out of it. That I was fortunate to be able to study and that self-pity would not help me in any way. Here I was, looking for empathy, and getting none of it. But it worked. It was a turning moment. My mindset changed. I started working less, but with more focus and I finished the year with my best results ever. I had received the proverbial kick-in-the-butt, which was exactly what I needed. Later in my career, I learned to embrace the tough love.'

So, it's clear. Tough love should be cherished. Do you have people who care enough to give you honest feedback with only your best interests at heart? Then keep them around, because you are incredibly lucky to have them. The way to do that is not by sucking up. That's not what a good mentor is looking for at all. Instead, be a sponge. Do something with the advice you are given. Show that you're willing to make an effort and make changes. There's nothing more discouraging for a mentor than having a mentee who's defensive and unwilling to take advice.

Tough love should be cherished. Do you have people who care enough to give you honest feedback with only your best interests at heart? Then keep them around.

Reciprocate the candor that they show you. You shouldn't feel like you need to perform a continuous good news show. As the saying goes: 'Good news needs to travel fast, and bad news even faster.' Be open and honest about the issues you face, and the doubts you have. You may be surprised by how much help and advice can come your way.

Feedback never stops

Being able to receive brutal feedback is not something you only need to do for a while. Sure, as long as you're at the bottom of the totem pole, you may think it's normal as there's so much you still need to learn. But even those who have made it to the top realize that they can only stay there if they remain open to feedback. That is because smart leaders are aware of CEO disease. As soon as you reach the top spot, you stop getting honest feedback. In order to fight that disease, CEOs have to organize their own opposition, starting with their own team of leaders. That means that the CEO, the team and the rest of the organization all have a barrier to overcome. The CEO must dare to be vulnerable and actively ask for feedback. The team and the other levels of the organization must dare to speak out honestly about the performance and decision-making of the man or woman at the top. Traditionally-minded CEOs often find it difficult to put themselves in that vulnerable position. They are afraid that asking for feedback will be seen as a sign of weakness. After all, the stereotype requires that leaders are charismatic, visionary, and have a monopoly on wisdom. But the stereotype is wrong. Because in fast-changing times, leaders need to develop as well. Mette Lykke actively solicits feedback from her team: 'I ask for feedback from my team. It's getting harder even though I don't think about us like a hierarchical organization but still, once you are the CEO many people are not comfortable giving feedback. But it's super important for the company I do not get stuck in my development. Especially in a fast- growing company. If you run a business that only grows 3-5%, what worked yesterday will probably work today as well. But here, we tripled in one year. Changes go fast, so I need to develop as well. One thing I learned for example is that I need to celebrate our achievements more with my team. Because I know that's a weakness of mine, we designed a workaround solution to compensate. We created this wall of achievements, and every time we hit one we do this ceremony where we officially unlock the achievement and drink the champagne.'

The CEO must dare to be vulnerable and actively ask for feedback.

What we know for sure

Recent research that Katleen conducted shows that it is not only charismatic and visionary CEOs who are successful: introverted top managers with a broadly supported and bottom-up vision can also be successful and book equally good business results. The research compared the effectiveness of CEOs with dominant visions with the effectiveness of CEOs who are more modest and ask for feedback from their co-directors. The research revealed that CEOs who ask for feedback from the people around them perform just as well as their visionary counterparts. In fact, they make optimal use of the strength of their team: the judgement and knowledge of their co-directors. Indirectly, that has a positive effect on the company's performance. The team members also gain more self-confidence and take a more proactive approach when the CEO systematically asks for feedback. After all, they do not have to wait or sit back and relax until the CEO has made the decision: they can actively influence the decision-making process. Moreover, the good example that is being set at the top of the company stimulates people at other organizational levels to ask for and give feedback, both within the walls of the company and outside. This feedback culture can also have a positive effect on the result, especially in the present age in which sharing and exchanging knowledge is becoming increasingly important to be able to make strategic shifts.

The research results show leadership in a different light: not only visionaries but also - and perhaps especially - modest and vulnerable CEOs can be good leaders. This has significant consequences for selection policy and leadership development. We will have to broaden the criteria by which we select (future) leaders and provide in-house training. A shift is already noticeable: the emphasis in training budding leadership talent has shifted towards the ability to work well with others rather than individual excellence. The 360-degree feedback tool is also used more and more frequently. In practice, however, more modest personalities who show vulnerability often still lose out to the macho types with the gift of gab in the rat race to the top. This suggests that a review of the assessment and remuneration policy is needed. This should not only look at the policy and results (what) but also the way this came about (how): to what extent did the leader ask for feedback from the people around them and focus on team performance?

Ashford, S., N. Wellman, M. Sully de Luque, K. De Stobbeleir, M. Wollan (2018). Two roads to effectiveness: CEO feedback seeking, vision articulation, and firm performance. *Journal of Organisational Behavior, 39 (1), 82-95.*

Take it from us

There is no bigger gift than to have people in your life who both believe in you and challenge you at the same time. The mentors you should value are those that know when to give you a pat on the back and when to kick your butt, and who do both out of love.

Let's put
the work
into your
network.

9 Know that you are the company you keep

The myth: careers are self-made

If you hang out with chickens, you're going to cluck, and if you hang out with eagles, you're going to fly.

Steve Maraboli

Networking. Some people truly enjoy it, while others dread the prospect of small talk with strangers. There's plenty of good advice on how to strike up a conversation at a networking event, or how to connect with a potential sales prospect. But there's much more to networking than exchanging business cards at a reception. Networking is as much about deepening the contacts you already have as it is about developing new contacts. This is also true with the people you actually see at work every day. It's mostly about realizing that you can't achieve anything without others, and that having different circles of people around you is crucial.

It's mostly about realizing that you can't achieve anything without others, and that having different circles of people around you is crucial.

Sure, you are smart, and hard-working, and persistent. So you think that you don't need to put in the work to schmooze with the right people in the right places. Your work just speaks for itself, right? If that's what you think networking is about, think again. No matter how self-made the business (wo)man, nobody can do it all on their own. And so the key question to ask yourself is: who will lift me up, and who will drag me down? Let's put the work into your network.

Cliques, phonies, and other baloney - the power of diversity

Opposites attract? Maybe in love, but in daily life you probably hang out the most with people just like you. When we get to choose, most of us prefer to connect with the same small group of people: our inner circle of trust. It may be a core crew of coworkers you eat lunch with, or maybe you have a "work spouse". But that's not enough. One of the caveats of a small circle of trust is that it becomes a circle of comfort. Especially when it becomes a place to voice complaints and merely offers the illusion of personal development. You may find a safe zone to openly complain about the decisions and actions taken by those outside of your clique and relish the "us versus the world" feeling, but that's not a recipe for constructive change.

One of the caveats of a small circle of trust is that it becomes a circle of comfort.

Our inner circle of trust is usually not very diverse and typically consists of people of the same age, the same gender, the same values, similar preferences and views ... a nice and safe group of like-minded people. That group actually resembles "cliques" from high school—a small group of best friends, who always look out for each other, and to whom you can openly talk about the daily stuff and gossip about people that don't belong to the clique. But we also know about the unhealthy dynamics that can emerge in a clique. When you're part of the "in crowd" you feel great, affirmed, and powerful. When you don't belong to the in-group you feel excluded and vulnerable. But don't fool yourself: effective networking has little to do with being in or out ... and it is just as tricky to be part of the in-group as it is to be "out". When you're part of an exclusive clique, your world view and perspective narrows and can even become an obstacle to your growth in the long term. In much the same way as children benefit from not always playing with the same friends, it is vital that, as a professional, you try to diversify your network. For example, our own research has shown that people who actively seek feedback from a wide variety of people are far more creative. So, successful networkers don't limit themselves to the same usual suspects who just confirm their own view of the world. They push themselves to find people who challenge their assumptions and dare to turn their worldview upside down.

In the inspiring podcast series "Zigo", Hans Bourlon, the CEO of Studio 100, remembers: 'Several years ago, I became the buddy of Abdi, a 14-year-old Somalian refugee. It turned out to be one of the most enriching experiences of my life—and I hope for Abdi too. You know ... when you see a lonely refugee, sitting there on the side of the road, looking at you with this sad face, you really don't have a clue. I never fully realized that behind that sad face there is actually just a young boy, who misses his mom, just like any 14-year-old who had to flee his country would miss his mom. It made me realize that we have more in common than we often think. Developing a relationship with Abdi really tested many of my assumptions. I vividly remember our discussions about why it was not ok for him to put erotic pictures on his Instagram, while it is perfectly ok to have paintings of naked women in your living room or a museum, or to have a tv show called "Temptation". How on earth do you explain that putting a picture on your Instagram is not ok, while watching Temptation and admiring a painting of a naked woman is socially accepted? I also remember how, for Abdi, it was just hilarious that we would drive up all the way to the Ardennes to go on a kayak trip or take a hike ... just for the fun of it ... He simply did not get why on earth you would walk or kayak from point A to point B, without any reason other than your own entertainment? Why would you waste your precious energy on something like that? Or why on earth would you go mountain biking—in circles, in the mud—to then go to a pub and have a drink? And you know what: I think he might be right. The things we find normal, that I used to find normal, are just as crazy when we start looking at them through the eyes of a 14-year-old refugee. Staying curious to other views and meeting people with completely different views, really has helped me to question my own assumptions.'

What we know for sure: leverage all your networks

If cliques can be dysfunctional, and staying an outsider doesn't work either, then what types of networks do we need? Herminia Ibarra and Mark Hunter recommend creating three types of networks. Your first network is a functional network of people you need and who help you to accomplish your work. Your second network is more developmental in nature and contains the people who help you in your personal growth and development. Your third network is strategic and can enable you to reach more long-term, strategic goals that are often beyond your immediate control.

So who's in your functional network? It may be your lunch buddy from IT who always has the latest news. Your desk colleague, who's always ready to help you out when you're stuck with something. Your team member, who you have developed a bit of a love/hate relationship with. You love his ability to stay upbeat, even when you need to pull long hours, but you hate that he has the uncanny ability to take credit for ideas that weren't his. So it's really those people that you interact with anyway when you are doing your job. Most of us are functional networkers, who create and use our network in order to be able to perform our core job well. Building a functional network comes pretty naturally, it's simply a byproduct of your job. So your functional network probably contains your team members, your supervisor, clients, etc. It's useful to ask yourself who you spend the most time with. Regardless of your role in your organization, it is very likely that you spend the least amount of time connecting with your peers (especially those in other departments). That's where you may be going wrong. Katleen's research shows that many of us underestimate the importance of building strong relationships with our peers. They are the ones whose help we need to get things done, to get additional resources ... even to get a promotion. There are even studies showing that your relationship with your peers is the best predictor of your career success. This also means that treating your peers as competitors is not typically the most desirable approach. Helena Buhr, a product manager at Spotify, emphasized the importance of peers when we interviewed her at the Spotify headquarters: 'Many people are focused on managing upwards and making a good impression on their bosses. But they forget about the importance of managing laterally and connecting with peers.' Power to the peers!

But optimizing your functional network is just the beginning. To really reap the benefits of building a network, you also need developmental and strategic networks. Your developmental network is the group of people with whom you can discuss your personal challenges; where you also allow yourself to be vulnerable without having to worry about prejudice. You may be part of a regular mentoring group. Or, if you're a woman, you may be part of a female leaders' network, where you can openly discuss the specific challenges you face as women. Tim Van Hauwermeiren, CEO of Argenx, advises people to think about a personal advisory board, a small group of people whom you trust with your anxieties and your ugliness.

That is why a strategic network is just as important. This is the type of network that will really push you out of your comfort zone, and which exposes you to things that are not in any way related to your current role or your personal development. A strategic network expands your perspective, and shows you that there is more to life and work than minding your own job. People in your strategic network allow you to see the bigger picture. And sometimes your network will give you the push you need to make an important decision. For example, Herman Van de Velde confesses that the Vlerick IGMO network, an intimate group of founders/owners of Belgian growth companies who help each other with personal and business issues, gave him the push he needed to bring his lingerie firm Van de Velde to the stock market.

Ibarra, H., and Hunter, M. (2007). How leaders create and use networks. *Growth*, *35*(1), 101-103.

De Stobbeleir, K., Ashford, S., and Zhang, C. (2020). Shifting focus: Antecedents and outcomes of proactive feedback seeking from peers. *Human Relations*, *73*(3), 303-325.

Give and take

Ok, so you have different people in your networks, and different networks around you to benefit from. But what do you really use your networks for? Some people think of their networks as a resource of people they can reach out to when they need it. But, really, that's not how it works. For example, it's not when you're out of a job that it's time to send mass messages to your LinkedIn network. And it's not when you want to ask his boss for a favor that it's a good time to reach out to that old classmate from college. Networking effectively is about proactively building lasting relationships.

Networking effectively is about proactively building lasting relationships.

When it comes to building relationships that last, Adam Grant, a leading professor at Wharton Business School, provides some excellent insights. In his book "Give and Take", he describes three different styles of how you can build relationships with others: a giving style, a taking style, and a matching style. So how do these styles work? Imagine the following situation, one that we're all familiar with: you need to get someone a birthday gift. But what, oh what, will you give? It will likely depend on your relational style. Suppose that you're a taker in the relationship. Very likely, you'll try to keep your investment as small as possible and seek to maximize your returns. You might give something that looks very impressive, but that actually took zero effort from you and that you may benefit from as well. Perhaps you'll give an expensive box of your favorite chocolates, knowing very well that this person doesn't eat chocolates and will share them with you. Or perhaps you'll give that ugly, but very expensive, laptop bag that you received from a client and that is lying around somewhere in a closet ... and you know what: let's leave the price tag on it so that the other person knows exactly what it cost. And that's the striking thing about a taking style: it often remains unnoticed because the other person is blinded by your apparent generosity. When you're a matcher in a relationship, your approach will likely be different. Probably, you'll first think of what you received for your birthday from this person, and then you'll find a gift that matches the value of the gift you received. You probably also keep a "favor account": when you do someone a favor, you ensure that at some point the favor gets returned to you. If you don't recognize yourself in either of these two styles, you might be a giver. As a giver, you're likely to invest quite some time and energy in thinking about what this person would really value. Perhaps you'll buy him those pink cowboy boots, while you actually hate both pink *and* cowboy boots. But what the heck, it's not your birthday but his, right? These relational styles also influence how we build and connect with our network ... and the extent to which it's built to last. Adam Grant's research shows very clearly that, in the long run, givers get the farthest. And interestingly, givers are not interested in being in the spotlight. Instead they are focused on helping others to become more successful. And the side effect is that they become visible by doing that. Obviously, you know plenty of examples that seem to prove the exact opposite: the "takers" who take advantage of the hard work of others. Or the "matchers" who keep a scorecard of favors. But Grant's research shows that even though a taking or matching style may be the fastest road to success, its success is short-lived. So instead of asking: 'What can my network do for me?', or 'Who owes me a favor?', think about how you can contribute to your network.

Mentors and sponsors

There are special kinds of givers that can supercharge your career: mentors and sponsors. These are the people that can really get you places. They speak from experience, and are only interested in giving back. A good mentor helps you to avoid the mistakes they made themselves, without imposing their own path on you. Cherish your mentors! How, you wonder? Well, the best way is to absorb their advice and feedback like a sponge, because there is nothing that gives a mentor more satisfaction than the feeling of really having helped someone.

Sponsors are a different breed. They are like super mentors. Not only are they there for you with good advice, but they also do more than that. They open doors and, if necessary, push you through them. Ilham Kadri, CEO of Solvay, always describes it like this: 'Mentors talk to you. Sponsors talk about you when you are not there.' Marion admits: 'Over the last 20 years I have benefited from quite a few mentors and sponsors. Some of my sponsors were also good mentors, as they were genuinely interested and were generous with their time and their advice. But some of the sponsors that had a huge impact were actually really bad mentors. Instead of giving advice, they just threw me in the deep end of the pool, confident that I would make it. They didn't always give me the most calming experiences, but they were hugely effective in pushing me forward and accelerating my learning curve.'

So, do you have a good mentor? Good. But if you can find yourself a sponsor, even better. And most importantly, pay it forward!

Your most important career decision

Ok, so we need to talk about it. Your relationship status. You put it on Facebook, but not necessarily on your CV. Nevertheless, your significant other may have a crucial impact on your career. Sheryl Sandberg does not beat around the bush about it. In her bestseller "Lean In", she writes: 'I truly believe that the single most important career decision a woman makes is whether she will have a life partner and who that partner will be.' And that statement is clearly not only true for women. We all have non-work relationships that influence our work identity. You may have friends you admire, or a sibling you can always turn to for advice. But the most powerful influence is the one you find at home. So why would you pretend that your career is entirely self-made? Although you may find that when two people give it all for their own goals, romance quickly makes way for a fight for dominance. In the search for your own equilibrium, you can easily step on each other's toes. And instead of walking forward hand in hand, it may feel more like each of you is pushing yourself to the forefront. It does not have to be that way. Be careful not to get stuck in a zero-sum logic of sacrifice and compromise, where only one person in a couple can thrive and the other just needs to tag along. There used to be this logic that each couple has a breadwinner–homemaker dynamic, with a clear split of roles where one is clearly the breadwinner and the other is the homemaker. But when both people in a couple have professional aspirations and personal dreams, it just does not work that way. Which does not make things easier. But it can make them infinitely more enriching. This is because you may find the biggest source of strength and inspiration very close to you. Katleen confirms the importance of your life partner: 'During my PhD I had the opportunity to study in the US for a year. I was very hesitant because I didn't want to keep my husband from his flourishing career. Manu noticed that I was holding myself back with feelings of guilt. He insisted that this was an opportunity of a lifetime and that I

'I truly believe that the single most important career decision a woman makes is whether she will have a life partner and who that partner will be.'

would regret it if we didn't go. So, he basically took a year off from work to be my plus one and join me in Michigan. He even joined a support group for spouses of expats. The support group didn't really know how to handle him, because all of their members were wives, not husbands. A few weeks later he joined an adventure club instead. We both got so much out of the experience. But I also realize that if I had chosen a different and less supportive life partner (or better: if he hadn't chosen me), my career path wouldn't have led me to the US.'

Take it from us

Careers are not entirely self-made. Yes, you do the lion's share of the work, but the people around you will have a significant impact on the extent to which your efforts pay off. So take note. Think about the people you surround yourself with. Fill your personal advisory board with people who have your best interests at heart and who dare to speak the truth.

Don't limit yourself to a small circle of trust. Many of us react allergically to the notion of networking because it feels unnatural, or even manipulative. Or we may refrain from it simply because we don't have the time. We confess, we too have a love-hate relationship with networking, especially when it comes to chitchat in the corridors. That's probably why we are often the last ones to find out about the latest office gossip. Over time, however, we've learned to think of it as building and maintaining sustainable relationships. Networking isn't about taking and thinking about what your network can do for you. Networking is about being generous and asking yourself what you can do for your network. And what goes around comes around.

Whether you like it or not, politics are a fact of life.

10 Make yourself visible

The myth: you need to play the game

When they go low, we go high.

Michelle Obama

'There are two types of people in this world: those who suck their way up, and those who work hard and stay invisible.' If this thought has ever crossed your mind, you probably have some first-hand experience of politics. You are working your a** off (pardon our French), only to see others getting all the credit. Such situations often leave us wondering whether we are fools, playing by the rules. Of all the themes that come up in our coaching sessions, politics are by far the most common. But, whether you like it or not, politics are a fact of life. They exist in every situation you can think of. Whether you're an actor trying to get a role, a writer craving a good review, a figure skater trying to get a spot on the Olympic team, or a volunteer who tries to contribute to the local hockey team ... wherever you find people, you will find politics. Even Aristotle pointed it out: 'Man is by nature a political animal.' We admit that we hate the smell

The key question is: is there a way to develop political skill without selling your soul? And, more importantly, how do you have fun in the process?

of office politics and when we see them we often feel tempted to call them out. After all, didn't Steve Jobs say: 'In weak companies, politics win. In strong companies, the best ideas do.' But the truth is, wherever you put a bunch of people together to achieve something, individual interests will soon start to rear their head and people will begin forming coalitions and jockeying for positions. It's a simple matter of human nature. So political savvy is a competence too and not all politics are necessarily bad. The key question: is there a way to develop political skill without selling your soul? And, more importantly, how do you have fun in the process? Let's talk politics: the good, the bad, and the ugly.

The good: politics are about impact

First the good news: humility pays off. You don't need to brag about your accomplishments in order to be accomplished. You may say that we are dreamers. After all, humility is not exactly the very first trait that comes to mind when you think of great business leaders such as Steve Jobs, Jeff Bezos, and Elon Musk. Luckily, we are not dreamers, but researchers. Our own research shows that CEOs who seek feedback, share information, and are willing to make joint decisions, lead firms that perform better.

Depriving the world of what you have to offer ... that would be the true shame!

But how can you even have an impact when you're humble? Isn't that a contradiction in terms? Don't humility and invisibility go hand in hand? Granted, invisibility always lurks around the corner when you are unpretentious ... after all, too much of a good thing can become a handicap. If you see modesty as a reason not to speak up and not to connect with others then you might enter the land of the invisible. And believe us, as introverted academics, we know the land of the invisible very well. It can be a bit of a frustrating land when you feel that the spotlight just never lands on you. But let's be honest: the land of the invisible can also feel comfortable. It's the land where you get to just work hard and keep your head down. Why would you put yourself out there, actively sharing your knowledge and ideas, attending events and receptions, polishing your personal brand and social media persona? It's easy to say that this is unnatural and shameful. But make no mistake: if that's your reasoning, you are just hiding. Depriving the world of what you have to offer ... that would be the true shame! So start seeing visibility and career advancement as a way of extending your reach and increasing your impact on society. And that's not selfish. It's a necessary step toward amplifying your contribution.

There are lots of ways to gain visibility whilst staying humble. At work, it could entail volunteering to make a presentation, speaking up in a meeting, interviewing a top expert, asking for feedback on something you've written, or simply having lunch with a senior leader. Or if you really don't like the spotlight, one of the best ways is to create visibility for other people. But visibility isn't only about work. We often underestimate the power of the things we do outside of work. The volunteering that we do, or the connections that we build through our hobbies.

Ultimately, visibility is about impact. In the land of the invisible, your impact will remain minimal. In order to have impact, you need to show up and speak up. And you need the support of others who could amplify your impact, for example, senior leaders, investors, or journalists. So sometimes you need to manage upwards, as much as you manage your relationships with peers and colleagues. But managing upwards is not about "sucking your way up" (so no, there's no need to tell your boss (s)he's a genius). It's simply about asking yourself how your ideas add value and showing your willingness to contribute.

The bad: politics that harm - the dark triad

Now let's not be naïve either. Bad politics do exist, and they are more prevalent than you think.

'Not all psychopaths are in prison – some are in the board room.' These were the legendary words spoken by the social psychologist Robert Hare in a lecture entitled "The Predators Among Us", in which he highlighted that psychopathic behavior is more common than we think. In the book "Snakes in Suits, When Psychopaths Go to Work", Robert Hare and Paul Babiak provide compelling evidence that psychopathic behavior is very much alive. And they tested their ideas using a very interesting sample: company board rooms. But we're sure that their findings can be extended into many contexts where people work together.

They were interested in finding out how a person who is bad-natured can accumulate so much power that they end up at the top of an organization, maybe even of an entire nation. Wouldn't there be any alarm bells that would stop them on their way up? Imagine a country where people can choose between 2 candidates to rule the nation. The first profile is a self-confident, seemingly reasonable, and quite charming individual, but underneath that mask is a selfish, manipulative, and dishonest person. The other option is an extremely competent individual, who is generous but also a bit aloof, rational, and brutally honest. Which one would you prefer? When you read the options like this, you'd probably say that you prefer none of them and that you'd pick a third option. Yet, astonishingly, regardless of the different options we get, in practice option one is the most prevalent. And that option comes close to what psychologists would call the dark triad personality profile, a profile that is associated with traits such as narcissism, Machiavellianism, and psychopathy. These traits come with one key characteristic: the tendency to exploit others. Hard to imagine someone like that? Think of Frank Underwood, the brilliant and charming, yet ruthless, politician played by Kevin Spacey in the Netflix series "House of Cards", who manipulates, bargains with, and pushes people until he gets what he wants, which is becoming the President of the United States. People with dark triad personalities are master chess players, focused on promoting their own status and power. And they are often so charming and manipulative that they can hide behind a well-cultivated mask of normalcy for years, and perhaps even for their entire lives. Their charm also often helps them to reach the upper echelons of organizations. So the chances are good that there is also a psychopath in the boardroom of your organization. Their tactics? They typically like to step into roles where the previous administrator screwed up and then make themselves indispensable, by creating an aura of seemingly effortless accomplishments around them. They are very skilled at generating visibility for themselves based on others' hard work and "forget" to give those others the credit they deserve. Surprisingly, though, these behaviors are rarely commented upon. They're usually too subtle and sneaky. And often you'll tell yourself that you're paranoid, and that you shouldn't be so sensitive. Or you may just be too scared to call them out. After all, dark triad personalities live by the mantra "hunt or be hunted".

Our advice? Take a very good look at what behaviors get rewarded in the organizations you engage with. If using your connections, charm, and yes-nodding get rewarded more than good ideas and debate, then this may be a sign of a highly politicized environment, especially if it's also an organization where people tend to stay in positions of power for a very long time. So pick your company well. Or better yet, become part of the solution. Like a gremlin, there's nothing that political people detest more than the direct sunlight. Transparency, clear and objective purposes, and open communication are your best weapons against a political environment.

What we know for sure: confidence often trumps competence

It's a stubborn puzzle for every advocate of more diversity at the top: why are there so few female leaders? Only about 5% of CEO's are women. Why is it so hard for competent and talented women to reach the top? Tomas Chamorro-Premuzic reversed the question by asking 'Why is it that it's so easy for incompetent men?' His answer to the disproportionate representation of women at the top is simple: it's because we are not good at recognizing leadership potential and have a misguided view of what leadership is about. We equate it with bravado and confidence. That means that people who display these external cues are seen as leadership material. We fall for charisma and extraversion, even narcissism. Because we've fooled ourselves into thinking that this is the picture of effective leadership.

Truth is, there is no basis for this. The best leaders are humble rather than charismatic, even somewhat boring. The leadership traits that lead to performance are integrity, competence and humility. Coincidentally, traits that often describe women's leadership style. But also traits that do not make them very visible as potential leaders.

In other words, we're just not very good at distinguishing between confidence and competence. And in selecting leaders, confidence often trumps competence. As a result, we select leaders based on the wrong set of criteria. (A certain presidential race between a brazen Donald Trump with no policy or government experience and a Hillary Clinton who had served just about in every capacity short of being the actual president, comes to mind).

Chamorro-Premuzic T. (2013). Why do so many incompetent men become leaders?. *Harvard Business Review*, 22 August 2013.

The ugly: does power corrupt?

As the English historian Lord Acton famously said, 'Power corrupts, and absolute power corrupts absolutely.' For decades, this was also the view held by psychologists. Think of the famous Stanford prison experiment, where students played the role of either prisoners or prison guards. Interestingly, all of the guards became abusive, and they took away the prisoners' clothes, forcing them to sleep on the cold floor. "Power corrupts" was the conclusion of this study, but one important detail was overlooked. The students who volunteered for the study were recruited from another "dark" experiment and displayed, on average, far more of the dark triad traits than would be found in the general population.

Today, psychologists agree that power corrupts those people who already lean toward corruption.

Of course, power can intoxicate even the most honest among us. Perhaps you won't ask people to sleep on the floor, but you may misuse your power in more acceptable ways. People in powerful positions have been shown to be three times more likely than others to say insulting things, to interrupt and manipulate others, and to abuse their power in order to generate visibility for themselves at the expense of others. This is especially true of the ones who have just gained such a position or who have been in those positions for too long, as they tend to get carried away by their power.

Power has an amplifying effect. Whoever you were before becomes amplified once you get a position of power. And the longer you stay in a powerful position, the darker those little edges will become, and the uglier things can get. Fortunately, some organizations have it in their DNA to break that cycle by preparing you for powerful positions, or by making it mandatory to rotate frequently so that you can't accumulate power. But even if your organization doesn't have such policies, it may actually be healthy to not stay in a powerful position forever. Build in frequent moments of reflection, take sabbaticals, and, most importantly, push yourself to reflect on how you want to use your power. Because, ultimately, you have a choice. You can use your power to benefit others or you can use your power for personal gain. The choice is yours.

What we know for sure: not all politics are bad

Luckily, not all politics harm others and there are ways to play the game without selling your soul to the dark triad. Politics is ultimately about understanding people and using that understanding to influence others, having your ideas be taken seriously and getting recognition for them. In that sense, politics aren't inherently good or bad, but it is how we use them that matters. Political skill consists of four key elements: (1) social astuteness, or the ability to read others; (2) interpersonal influence, or the ability to influence what other people think; (3) networking ability, or the capacity to form mutually beneficial relationships with a variety of people; and (4) apparent sincerity: seeming to be honest, open, and forthright. The last one, especially, is quite intriguing. It's not about being honest, it's about how honest others think you are, and those are different things. It's the difference between being right and being righteous.

These skills are unrelated to your intelligence, and when you develop them, you can strengthen your impact, job performance, and career advancement. Research also shows that a failure to develop these skills in a highly politicized environment can derail the career of even the most intelligent, honest, and hard-working people.

Kaiser, R., Chamorro Premuzich, T. and Lusk, D. (2017). Playing Office Politics Without Selling Your Soul. *Harvard Business Review*, September 2017.

Showing up without showing off

Virtually everyone has experienced situations where they have worked hard and still ended up missing out on an interesting project or an interesting opportunity you really wanted to land. According to Laura Huang, the author of "Edge", ultimately, it's about our ability to provide value and enrich those around us. We need to define our "edge"—the unique qualities that set us apart—and take strategic steps to make sure that other people see our value and open the doors that will take us where we want to go. That said, if you have something to bring to the table, you also need to demonstrate and effectively communicate the value you bring, rather than leaving it up to others to guess. You need to work hard, but when so many decisions are driven by the outside perceptions of others, you need to learn to identify what these perceptions are, how they operate, and the assumptions that people are making about your character and abilities. That will allow you to allocate effort, and that includes effort toward understanding how to operate to gain visibility for yourself and your ideas. You shouldn't just let others' views of your capabilities or limitations hold you back. So do show and tell, that does not make you a show-off.

Take it from us

We're told that the secret to success is hard work. But the truth is that hard work alone won't do the trick. Granted, life would be so much simpler if everyone was just focused on getting the job done, whatever that job entailed. But the reality is that when your only focus is results, it will become difficult to have any sort of impact down the road. Ultimately, you isolate yourself if you keep your head down. Effective politicians are not focused on stealing the spotlight from others. They use their political savvy to connect with others and create more impact with their ideas.

Leadership is a daily choice.

11 Take the lead

The myth: you're either a natural born leader or just not meant to be one

If not me, who? If not now, when?

Emma Watson

What are the first words you think of when we ask you to describe a great leader? Most people use words such as "smart", "charismatic", and "visionary". And they also mention such people as Steve Jobs. This mental model that we have of leadership puts it at an unreachable level of competencies and traits. It's time to get rid of this viewpoint. It's outdated, and very unproductive. And it makes legions of highly talented people believe that they are simply not leadership material. Who thinks of him- or herself as charismatic and visionary anyway? So, can anyone become a leader? If you define a "leader" as someone who runs a company or leads a team, then maybe the answer is no. But is that what leadership is about? A job title? If there is one thing we know for sure, it is that leaders come in many shapes and sizes. So stop asking yourself the questions, 'Am I a leader? Do I have what it takes?' Instead ask yourself, 'What kind of leader am I?' Ultimately, the real challenge that rests on

So stop asking yourself the questions, 'Am I a leader? Do I have what it takes?' Instead ask yourself, 'What kind of leader am I?'

your shoulders is to become the kind of leader you aspire to be. So what will be your choice?

Practice makes perfect

'(S)he's a natural born leader.' It's one of the greatest compliments you can get in life—but it's bollocks. What makes Indra Nooyi (former PepsiCo CEO) great? What made Steve Jobs great? We often think they came into the world with a special gift: leadership. But it's not that simple. It turns out that the vast majority of so-called "natural" leaders are made through deliberate and focused effort. Gary Player, one of the greatest golf icons of all time, said it nicely: 'The harder I practice, the luckier I get.' Management guru Malcolm Gladwell has even put a figure on the number of hours of work that are needed to become a success in any field: 10,000 hours.

Warren Bennis spent his entire career studying leaders and leadership. His conclusion was quite simple: 'Biographies of great leaders sometimes read as if they entered the world with an extraordinary genetic endowment, as if their future leadership role was preordained. Do not believe it. The most dangerous leadership myth is that leaders are born – that there is a genetic factor to leadership.' The truth is that you can practice many elements of leadership without having a formal leadership role. Presenting, negotiating, giving feedback, reading financial statements—you can practice them all. Of course, there is more to leadership than that. Can you also learn how to inspire or how to be empathic? Can you become charismatic just by practicing? Actually, yes. While a skill such as empathy can come instinctively to some, but is more elusive for others, research by Harvard professor Helen Riess shows that it can actually be taught. Helen Riess found that many physicians are toughened by their education and by their jobs. Nevertheless, they can be trained to be more empathic with their patients. And when you read Steve Jobs' biography carefully, you can only conclude that he had to learn many leadership skills the hard way. In the eighties, he got himself kicked out of his own company because of his "lack of leadership". He was just too difficult to work with. Less than fifteen years later he became a leadership legend. The rest is history. If you ask a leader you look up to about how they became the leader they are today, the answer will rarely be that they were born with a unique set of talents. Instead, they'll tell you stories of their personal struggles and the difficulties they had as they learned how to lead. Even Walt Disney was fired by an editor because 'he lacked imagination and had no original ideas.' And that might just have been the push he needed to work harder. Roch Doliveux, former CEO of UCB, a global pharmaceutical company, confesses: 'I never thought that I was going to become a CEO. And for a really long time throughout my career I felt an outsider. As a veterinarian, I already did not have the typical background of a business person. And I also felt I was too much of a softie to be a CEO. I doubted myself for a long time. Even at my retirement party, I kept thinking I did not really deserve the accolades but only got lucky. But in truth everybody has potential. You just have to trust that and be willing to discover your own potential. Doubting yourself is actually a good way to realize this, because it keeps you humble and it's a source of progress as you keep on questioning yourself and improving yourself.'

Why should anyone be led by you?

Why should anyone be led by you? It's not an easy question to answer, not even for established bona fide leaders. Of course, we can't all become the same type of people as Steve Jobs, Martin Luther King Jr., or Barack Obama. But we can learn to leave a positive mark. And the truth is, you can lead in one way or another, no matter what your position is. The CEO who leads from the front is a leader. But so is the factory worker who guides a colleague. Or the expert who transfers his/her expertise to others. In fact, you can even lead by being someone's first follower. In an inspiring TED talk, Derek Sivers highlights how being someone's first follower can make all the difference between leaving someone standing alone and starting an entire movement. So, basically, everyone is born to lead. And everybody can be a leader. Leadership is a daily choice. It's about your impact, and about the amount of growth, empowerment, courage, and self-respect that you demonstrate every day. And that's why you should lead. And everybody has the capacity to create those acts. If you think about it, the thought that all of us can lead is actually quite liberating. If you believe that there can only be one leader, then leadership becomes something to compete for and is seen as something that only the happy few can achieve. But if you believe that leadership can be shared and isn't positional, you'll respond much more collaboratively to those who dare to show leadership. We can't all be effective leaders all the time, or leaders who get all the spotlight. But what we know for sure is that when you stay in your comfort zone, your leadership potential will remain hidden.

Everyone is born to lead.

'I can't lead because I'm not the manager.' 'I am an introvert, I'm just not a natural take-charge person.' These are only a few of the reasons (or excuses?) that people use to keep their leadership potential hidden. But do you really need to be "the boss" to show leadership? If Martin Luther King had believed that, then he probably wouldn't have started a movement that spoke to the problems of so many African Americans. And if introverts can't lead, then Bill Gates, a self-proclaimed introvert, would have remained a hidden figure to all of us. The reality is that leading is scary. Fear of criticism, fear of failure, fear of making decisions, fear of speaking up, fear of responsibility ... fear is always there to greet us.

These are just a few of the fears that come with leadership. Whatever your fear is, don't strive to be more fearless. That's an illusion. Face your fear head on. In her book "The Art of Fear", Kristen Ulmer, once recognized as the best extreme skier in the world (jumping off cliffs and the whole shebang), argues that it's not the fear itself that makes us shy away from achieving great things. Instead, it's our misguided reaction to fear that paralyzes us. If you avoid fear, you get bored and complacent and you'll never grow. If you embrace it, you'll push yourself out of your comfort zone. Every decision you make comes with this type of conflict—a type of conflict that psychologists call approach-avoidance conflict. Andrew Elliot and Ken Sheldon have pioneered a great deal of research about approach and avoidance. Their research shows that when you avoid your fear, this will lead to decreased self-esteem and feelings of incompetence, but if you find a way to channel your fear, you'll shine like a star.

In the face of fear, consider the approach that Bertie takes in the award-winning movie "The King's Speech". The movie stars Colin Firth as King George VI of England (King Bertie), who needs to overcome a severe speech impediment. The stakes are extremely high, as the country is close to war, making public speaking an essential part of the King's role. Instead of avoiding his worst nightmare, Bertie confronts his fear of public speaking by seeking the help of Lionel Logue, a speech therapist. The end of the movie is about as good as it gets. Even though Bertie isn't fully cured of his stammer and still needs Logue to guide him, by the end he is speaking freely.

If you avoid fear, you get bored and complacent and you'll never grow. The magic happens when you're out of your comfort zone.

So be brave and confront your fears: the magic happens when you're out of your comfort zone.

What we know for sure: perks, privileges, and paychecks are not the best motivation

In order to conquer your leadership fears, it's important to ask yourself why you want others to follow you. People assume the leadership mantle for three key reasons. Some of us lead because we just enjoy the process of leading others, and have a strong desire to lead. We take the lead because of the pleasure and personal satisfaction it brings. Think of the kid in the playground that was already bossing everyone around as the leader of the pack. That was the kid we all wanted to be because (s)he had it all: the looks, the cool parents, the social skills, and the great results, both at school and in extracurricular activities. While such an intrinsic motivation may seem like the perfect basis for leadership, for many of us leadership is about more than just the satisfaction of taking the lead. It also comes with a responsibility. Instead of seeing leadership as something "fun", some of us lead out of a sense of moral duty or social obligation. Greta Thunberg isn't that popular kid in the playground. She just sees it as her moral duty to stand up and lead. Politicians often project this motivation for leadership (or they pretend to). 'I'm taking responsibility because I was asked to by the people.' Finally, some of us take a more calculative approach to leadership, and only step up when we have a clear answer to the question: "What's in it for me?". Those types of leaders are drawn to the perks, privileges, and paycheck that may come with having a position of leadership, and carry the burden of the work and the responsibility only when there are enough other benefits. Research also shows that your answer to the question "Why do you lead?" impacts how well you'll lead. For many, the reason why they lead is, of course, a mix of intrinsic motivations (e.g., the obligation to serve and the joy of leading) and extrinsic ones (e.g., career progress and status). However, a study by Amy Wrzesniewski from Yale, who tracked leaders over a 14 year period, showed that those who led for both internal and external reasons were far less effective leaders than those who are motivated from within.

Chan, K.Y. and F. Drasgow. (2001). Toward a Theory of Individual Differences and Leadership. *Journal of Applied Psychology,* 83 (3), 481-498.

Wrzesniewski, A., Schwartz, B., Cong, X., Kane, M., Omar, A., and Kolditz, T. (2014). Multiple types of motives don't multiply the motivation of West

Point cadets. *Proceedings of the National Academy of Sciences, 111(30)*, 10990-10995.

When duty calls–the leadership journey of Catherine Gilain-Pycke

We interviewed Catherine Gilain-Pycke, CEO of the fourth generation dairy company Inex. In an incredibly authentic conversation, Catherine described how, in 2000, she unexpectedly became the CEO of Inex at the age of 37, and how 20 years later she is reflecting on her legacy and making a new transition: the transition to the next generation. 'Unfortunately my father passed away early and unexpectedly. Being the oldest child and the most ready to take over his role, I became CEO of Inex when he became ill. I had just turned 37 at the time. I was not at all prepared, even though I had a good knowledge of the company. There was not an enormous amount of time to think it all through. I really felt like it was my responsibility toward not only our coworkers and the more than 500 farmers who have delivered their milk to us for generations. I was a CEO for 3 years while my father was still alive. I must say this was the worst period of my life. He was sick and depressed, but still wanted to be closely linked to the company. It made good people leave and sent our activities into a negative spiral. It was very sad to see a person like my father, who made Inex what it still is today, destroying what he had built during his whole career. During the 10 years following the dioxine crisis in 1999, which hit us very hard (we lost 30% of our turnover in 1 day), we have been working to rebuild what was lost. During that time I have been very supported by both my siblings and some good and dedicated colleagues who had the same objective as the 4th generation, to get Inex back on track. It was just duty calling.'

Beware of the glass cliff!

While it may be commendable to dutifully take on the leadership role when someone needs to step up to the plate, women especially need to be aware of the glass cliff. The term, coined by University of Exeter professors Michelle Ryan and Alex Haslam, is used to describe situations in which women are appointed to leadership roles during a crisis situation or chaotic moment, when the odds of success are low. Because men have a stronger tendency to refrain from taking the lead at these times, women get the opportunity to fill the void. Theresa May is a perfect example. Only the second woman to take on the role of prime minister of the UK, she came into the position during a particularly turbulent period. It happened because her predecessor resigned right after the British population voted, quite unexpectedly, in favor of Brexit (meaning the UK should leave the European Union). None of the political leaders who had supported Brexit were eager to come to the forefront once the vote was final. It was clear that the Brexit vote had been won only by a narrow margin. And while the idea of separating from the European Union was simple in theory, executing it in practice was surely going to be a difficult task. And so Theresa May became the fallback leader, as none of the men stepped up. A few excruciatingly difficult years later, Theresa May resigned. With the finishing line in sight, Boris Johnson, who had advocated for Brexit all along, took over.

So, ladies, when duty calls, beware of taking on a mission impossible, only to be set up to fail! Make sure you have the necessary backing and a good plan. And you may just surprise friend and foe, and make it after all!

Take it from us

Yes, you can lead. This is because leaders are made, not born. Our proposition is not groundbreaking. A leader is someone we follow voluntarily, not because they have the job title. Leaders come in all shapes and sizes, and there are many different and important ways to be a leader. Mastering a new skill requires you to conquer some of your fears. And leadership is no different. So dare to show up and take responsibility. Don't wait until you have the formal position or power to be a leader. It's common sense, but not common practice.

The only way to completely master it is to actually do it.

12 Get into the arena

The myth: before I take on a challenge I need to make sure I'm competent

I'm now a grown-up myself. I feel like I've been promoted beyond my competence.

Pamela Druckerman

David came to ask for advice. He was a hard-working and talented software developer. He really loved his job, working for a fast-growing and born global company. There were always new projects to work on, and the company was very supportive in allowing him to keep on top of new developments in his field and learn new things. The biggest satisfaction he got was from seeing new features that he had worked on go live and become part of the product. The atmosphere in his team was pretty casual. People worked quite hard, but nobody was very strict about when and where the job got done. David loved the flexibility to come in as he wished and dress as he wanted. His colleagues had become good friends, and going into the office every day did not really feel like work. But now he had been approached to take on a new role. It was an exciting opportunity that would allow him to discover a new area within the company, and he would also get a significant pay raise. But he also felt very unsure about it. The new role would entail a lot more customer-facing work. He would have to discuss with customers what their specific requirements were, and be responsible for implementing customer projects from start to finish. David felt really honored to be approached for the role. But was he really cut out for it? He knew he had the technical skills. But this was a much more people-oriented and commercial role, which were two elements that he had very little experience in. Was he too much of an introvert to thrive in such a job? Would he have the necessary diplomatic and negotiation skills needed to navigate the minefield of translating customer requirements with complex decision-making units? And did he really want to leave his current team? He was in his element and felt very comfortable in his current job. Why would he want to give that up and stretch himself by going into the unknown?

You may recognize David's predicament. Taking on a new role may feel much more like a leap into the unknown than an easy step forward on stable ground. And you may not feel ready for it. Not yet. If only you could prepare yourself a bit more. Gain a bit more experience. Take a course first. Surely you don't know everything you need to know yet. And you don't yet have all that it takes.

But, see, that is always a part of taking on a new challenge. You can never be fully prepared. And you will never already have everything that it takes. But maybe everything you need is already inside you, ready to blossom and flourish with the right fertilizer. Think about when you first learned to drive a car. Sure, you can read the car manual or watch a YouTube video. But there is just no alternative to getting into the actual car for the first time,

You will never already have everything that it takes.

starting up the engine, and getting it moving. With a patient person next to you to guide you, you probably managed to take that first spin without too much harm. The first time on the road on your own may have felt exhilarating and scary. By now, you probably don't even have to think about all of the steps involved, and you do it all on autopilot. But who wants to live life on autopilot? Let's take the more exhilarating ride.

That is what is happening with any new challenge you take on. The only way to completely master it is to actually do it. You can never be fully competent before taking on a new role. And as difficult and exciting as your new role may feel in the beginning, there will come a time when it will all become routine, maybe even boring! But, to get there, you do need to take the leap, fully knowing that you do not currently have all of the competencies it takes, but that you will develop them quickly enough as you go along. Because, the thing is, sitting on the sidelines does not make you more able to go onto the field. Paul Bulcke: 'Taking on a new challenge always contains risk, and you ask yourself "Am I ready for this?"'. But even something as simple as walking requires that you lift one foot up and for a split second you're only balancing on one foot. Imbalance is part of moving forward. Over time, you're ready to climb bigger and bigger hills, and then mountains. So Aretha Franklin was right: Ain't really no mountain high enough!

The only way to completely master it is to actually do it.

Imposter syndrome

Even once you are on top of the mountain, you may not necessarily feel that you belong there. That feeling of not deserving your spot on that mountain is what is called the imposter syndrome. It manifests itself as a nagging voice in your head, telling you that you do not deserve your success, and if people knew the reality of your incompetence then you would be on your way out in a heartbeat. Yes, even highly accomplished people suffer from imposter syndrome and the fear of being exposed as a "fraud". Sheryl Sandberg, COO of Facebook, wrote about it extensively in her book "Lean In". Even she, arguably one of the most successful and accomplished women on this planet, suffers from imposter syndrome. Go figure! Yes, even those who are publicly applauded can still feel as though everybody applauding them is actually making a mistake. When Jodie Foster won an Oscar, the highest recognition an actor can ever wish to achieve, she acknowledged later on that it felt like a fluke: 'I thought everybody would find out, and then they would take the Oscar back.' When you receive public recognition it can feel unnerving. Achieving the success you have been dreaming about can feel great, but it can also throw you off-balance a bit. This is because you are trying to reconcile the image you have of yourself with the image that others have of you. Only you are entirely privy to the hard work, the self-doubt, the mistakes, the humble first steps, the setbacks, and the failed attempts that were part of your journey. Being fully in the know about the often invisible hard side of success makes you humble about your own abilities. And to achieve applause can then feel undeserving. Just know that others who receive applause are facing the same struggles that you do. It's just that you can only see the results they achieve, without seeing the blood, sweat, and tears that have been part of it for them. Always remember that the outside image is never the full story, and that others' success does not come as easily as it may appear.

Marion confesses: 'The first time I heard about imposter syndrome, it was a huge a-ha-moment. Before that, I really thought I was the only person in the world that was walking around in her professional environment with the secret fear of being "unmasked". It was during my first years as a professor in the US. It had been really thrilling to sign my first contract as a professor, but deep down I felt like those people offering me the job were clearly making a mistake. Surely they could not really believe that this girl from Belgium was qualified to teach those smart and driven MBA students, who were mostly older than me? And they could not honestly believe that I had all the necessary training and the background to be a real professor? Clearly, there would come a moment that they would realize that I actually did not belong there. But the first year, nothing of the sort happened, I even got a raise. And the second year, it did not happen either. Although I did continue to have this feeling deep down that I was faking it. That I was the fraud amongst the "real" professors, who actually knew what they were doing. And then I stumbled across a piece on imposter syndrome. It turns out that many people walk around in their professional environment feeling like they are just pretending to know what they are doing.'

Marion's experience is one that many competent women and men will recognize. In fact, approximately 70% of people experience imposter symptoms at some point in their life. Why not consider your imposter syndrome as a slightly annoying, but dear, friend? Because as much as you may loathe the feeling of not belonging, there are advantages to feeling this way. Suffering from imposter syndrome indicates that you're challenging yourself. When things are new, we don't feel as comfortable as when we are doing something that we've been doing for the last 15 years. And you aren't growing as a human being if you aren't pushing yourself outside your comfort zone. Your imposter syndrome also keeps your ego in check; feeling like an imposter can be a good thing because it won't allow your ego to become overinflated. When your ego takes over, you tend to get comfortable and avoid potential unknowns. This way, you won't take opportunities for granted and will be open to learning new things so that you can continue to sharpen your skills and experience. And finally, suffering from imposter syndrome may mean that you're becoming smarter. There's a famous quote from Aristotle, 'The more you know, the more you know you don't know.' Several experts believe that imposter syndrome arises as a result of becoming more accomplished at what you do. Basically, it could be a sign that you are learning more and getting better at your craft, which is something to celebrate. That said, if you don't have the imposter syndrome, don't worry. Because ultimately, the imposter syndrome is damaging, both for yourself and for your environment. Feelings of inadequacy may lead to self-sabotaging behaviors that turn fears into realities.

Or you may feel compelled to start pretending as if you know everything, even if you don't.

If you really want to get rid of that annoying friend called imposter syndrome, here's what to do. Recognize imposter feelings when they emerge. Awareness is the first step to change, so ensure that you track these thoughts: what are they and when do they emerge? Then rewrite your inner dialogue (you know, that conversation with yourself that's always going on inside your head). Instead of telling yourself that you will be uncovered as a fake, or that you don't deserve success, remind yourself that it's normal not to know everything and that you're just learning. And don't keep the dialogue to yourself. Talk about your feelings. There may be others who feel like imposters too—it's better to have an open dialogue rather than harbor negative thoughts alone. Be kind to yourself. Remember that you are entitled to make small (and even big!) mistakes and forgive yourself. Don't forget to celebrate the wins and achievements, not only the big ones but also the small ones.

The power of asking for help

'There's no such thing as a stupid question,' well-meaning teachers often shout out. Deep down, though, you may beg to differ, especially if you feel like a faker anyway. When you suffer from imposter syndrome, the last thing you want to happen is to be found out. So you hide your feelings of incompetence really well, so that nobody figures out that you don't really know what you are doing. A person suffering from imposter syndrome will try to keep up the charade and does not ask any questions or advice from others. But an important lesson for anyone to learn is that you cannot do it alone, and that asking for input and advice from others does not make you look any less capable. In fact, it only makes you look better!

Marion admits, 'It's a lesson I took a long, long time to learn. And, in fact, if there was a single thing I could go back and change about myself in my early career, it would be that I would turn myself into a serial questioner. How much agony and needless suffering I could have saved myself from!' Why do we find it so hard to ask for help from other people? When tackling a challenge, you may think you need to show that you can do it alone. But that strategy backfires more often than not. Wanting to do things by yourself, without considering any input from others, makes you more likely to look like a stubborn fool instead of a solitary genius.

What we know for sure:
asking for advice makes you seem more competent

When you ask for advice before completing a task, you are perceived as being more competent, not less!

A series of studies published in Management Science explores the effect that seeking advice has on the advice seeker's perceived competence. The results convincingly busted a few of the biggest myths about asking for advice. First of all, asking for advice does not make you seem less competent. On the contrary, when you ask for advice before completing a task, you are perceived as being more competent, not less! This happens irrespective of the performance you show when completing the task itself. Of course, good advice would normally help you to achieve a better result, but on top of that you will be perceived as more competent simply because you asked for advice.

Why does this happen? Well, think about when somebody asks you for advice on a subject. It's flattering for your ego, right? That ego boost you get from being asked for your input makes you look more favorably toward the one asking you for advice, and hence you view them as more competent.

What if you're asking for advice about something simple? Would that not make you seem stupid? As if you cannot accomplish even the simplest thing by yourself? No. There is nothing to be feared. Asking for advice does not make you seem less competent, even when the task you are asking for advice on is simple. Furthermore, asking for advice about a difficult task makes you seem even more competent. So there is only an upside to asking for advice.

What if you ask the wrong person for advice? Would that not make you seem stupid? Again, there is nothing to be feared. You will not be seen as less competent if you ask for advice from a person who does not know a lot about the subject.

So, in conclusion, if you face a difficult challenge, then go ahead and ask for advice from knowledgeable people. They will only think you're more competent because of it.

Brooks, A.W., F. Gino, and M. Schweitzer. (2015). Smart People Ask for (my) Advice: Seeking Advice Boosts Perceptions of Competence. *Management Science,* 61 (6), 4121-1435.

A special word for the girls

It's a well-known fact that men apply for a job when they meet 60% of the qualifications, but women only apply when they are sure they meet all of the requirements. Girls often need the extra push to go for it. Even when we are qualified, we often need to be asked instead of pursuing an opportunity ourselves. Have we read too many fairy tales and watched too many Disney movies, so we've become convinced that opportunities will show up to swoop us away like a prince on a white horse, meaning that we don't need to go after them ourselves? Let's not make the same mistakes so many women have made before us.

From an early age, girls are being expected to play by the rules. While boys are usually expected to be a little mischievous in getting their way, girls are taught to be good. At the age of 5, Katleen's daughter Lune got a comment at summer camp that she had to learn to color more neatly within the lines of her coloring book, because this 'is especially important for a girl'. And given that girls are taught to be perfect, we also try to be ... perfect! We do as we are told, try to gain the approval of our parents and teachers, and work diligently to get good grades. This has led to a good level success, as girls now make up the majority of university students and achieve excellent results. But once they enter the workforce something changes. At the time of graduation, women and men are equally ambitious, and equally convinced that they will be able to gain leadership positions. But a couple of years later, that has changed. Women store their ambitions, and become less convinced that they are attainable.

Surely, there's a lot that could happen inside organizations to create an environment that generates equal opportunities for both genders—and there's no reason why we can't have the ambition to create these for ourselves.

At school, the only thing you need to do is study and do well on exams and written papers. There's not a lot of self-promotion involved. And good work will be recognized as good work, because everybody needs to pass the same tests. Once you enter the workforce, that changes. Your good work will not be noticed automatically. You'll need to put in some extra work in order to create relationships with those people that can help you move forward. And you will need to make sure that your contributions are known and visible. You may feel that bragging is not a good tactic. Women, especially, feel uncomfortable advertising their own accomplishments. And they're partially right, because women face a penalty for self-promotion that men don't. But slaving away out of the limelight is also not particularly helpful. There are certainly ways to put your work in the spotlight without being seen as a shameless self-promoter. Framing your work in the sense of how it helps to achieve a common goal is one effective way to do it. And, in any case, don't be the pushover who takes on the office housework! You know the type of tasks. The things that need to be done, but are not particularly newsworthy. The invisible work that needs to be done but which isn't critical enough to get you that promotion: organizing the holiday party, helping newbies navigate the place, taking notes at a team meeting, filling in when a colleague is absent, etc. Women volunteer more than men for tasks like these, and they are also more frequently asked to do them (not because women are appreciated more for doing this type of work, but because the people asking have a hunch that there is a lower chance that a woman will turn it down, a hunch which is right). So instead of leaning in, just lean back when office housework needs to be done. Focus on that work that is strategically important and core to the business, and you will definitely be noticed. And how to cope with stereotypes? Sometimes humor can help. Katleen relates: 'Luckily, I have never experienced explicit forms of discrimination. But of course people have biases. Several years ago, I taught my very first class for a senior group of executives. I arrived very early to make sure that everything was perfect. Also one of the participants came in early. Not realizing that this thirty-something lady would be his professor for the day, he asked: 'Honey, could you get me a coffee?' I simply said: 'Of course, sir, just give me a minute'. He drank his coffee without giving the incident any further thought. But inside I felt humiliated. When I started my session, he realized his error and turned completely red. During the break he kept on apologizing and we had a good laugh about it. I think he learned a valuable lesson, but so did I. I learned about the power of humor'.

What we know for sure: don't use the humblebrag

How can you boast about your accomplishments and still come across as sympathetic? You may have used the humblebrag on occasion. You know the type of thing: 'Goodness, there's no way I'll ever find the time to answer all of these congratulatory messages!' or 'Can't believe they're giving this important industry award to me, it must have been slim pickings for the jury this year'.

There is no denying it, humblebragging is bragging alright, but it's bragging masked as something else. Professor Sezer from Harvard Business School investigated what types of humblebrag exist and whether or not they really work. She found that humblebragging is a self-presentation strategy that aims to fulfil a dual purpose: highlighting your positive qualities and appearing competent, but at the same time eliciting sympathy and seeming likable. She found that there are two types of humblebrags. One type masks the brag with a complaint, e.g., 'It's so hard to deal with all of the attention I get', 'People can never seem to believe you can be beautiful and still be smart!' The other type masks the brag with humility, e.g., 'I can't believe they gave this important project to me'.

It turns out that both types of humblebrags are ineffective. They don't make you seem more competent, and neither do they make you seem more likable than if you just plainly brag.

So don't use humility to mask your bragging, it's better to just tout your accomplishments as they are. And don't use complaints to mask them either. Either complain or brag, but don't hide one behind the other.

Sezer, O., F. Gino, and M.I. Norton (2018). Humblebragging - a Distinct and Ineffective Self-presentation Strategy. *Journal of Personality and Social Psychology*, 114(1), 52-74.

You may be hesitant to put your own work in the spotlight because you actually think it's not all that noteworthy or exceptional. Do know that this is a trap you are stepping into. Women tend to be less confident about their own abilities, especially when they are young. But also know that being overly confident may actually be a bigger trap than underestimating your own abilities. This is because when you're not sure how you will tackle a challenge, you will ask for more advice and input. You will consider more alternative scenarios. You will ask more questions. And you will seek to constantly do better. All are powerful, positive drivers. So if you're not feeling fully confident, think of this as the push that will drive you to do better.

And finally, know that the rule book for the real world still needs to be written. So playing nicely by the rules is not going to get you far. Do you know why women only apply for a job when they can fulfil all of the requirements that are written down in the job posting? It is because we tend to assume that those rules will actually be followed, and that the chosen person needs to check all of the boxes. In reality, the job description is mostly only a wish list and probably even wishful thinking. Men, having learned from a young age to bend the rules a little, simply assume that there will be some wiggle room.

Take it from us

There is no guaranteed recipe for success. The only way to achieve anything great will be to take a risk and go for it at some point. Rest assured that you will not always feel sure of yourself. And as you leap into the unknown, you may fail. But know that you will probably always regret more the risks you did not take than the ones you did. And as there will always be people on the sidelines who will tell you 'I told you so', it may be good to keep in mind the words of Theodore Roosevelt:

'It is not the critic who counts;
not the man who points out how the strong man stumbles,
or where the doer of deeds could have done them better.
The credit belongs to the man who is actually in the arena,
whose face is marred by dust and sweat and blood; who strives valiantly;
who errs, who comes short again and again,
because there is no effort without error and shortcoming;
but who does actually strive to do the deeds;
who knows great enthusiasms, the great devotions;
who spends himself in a worthy cause;
who at the best knows in the end the triumph of high achievement,
and who at the worst, if he fails,
at least fails while daring greatly...'

So dare to enter the arena! Because the only way you deserve to challenge the world is to challenge yourself first.

Can only the thick-skinned make it?

13 Be courageous (and thus vulnerable)

The myth: it's all strictly business

You can choose courage or you can choose comfort. You cannot have both.

Brené Brown

"It's not personal, it's just business." Yeah, right. There is only one place where this sentence belongs, and that's in the movie "The Godfather". Other than that, let's wipe it from our business lingo altogether.

Perhaps you would never (ever) rush off to the bathroom and cry your eyes out after a particularly difficult conversation with a colleague. Perhaps you never feel the urge to release your frustration by throwing darts at the picture of someone who has treated you badly. After all, you are a true and thick-skinned professional who can deal with a sneer or two. True professionals don't allow their emotions to get the better of them. It *is* just business, right? So perhaps this chapter doesn't really apply to you. But perhaps you feel a little pull to read it anyway. Not for yourself, of course, but for a good friend of yours who does get emotional sometimes. Maybe you have already advised your friend to develop a thick skin and not to take things so personally.

Well-intended advice, the type of advice you would also get from a coach or a mentor. But maybe it's not the best advice you'll ever get—sorry, the best advice to give to your (imaginary?) good friend.

Somehow, we are conditioned to believe that emotions are less legitimate than thoughts, so we pretend that we are never affected by them ... and we tell others not to let themselves be affected by them either. But should you really suppress your emotions? Is it impossible to think rationally if you are emotional? Or do emotions have a place in the workplace after all? Newsflash: actually, you can't think rationally if you are not emotional.

Even Jack Welch, aka Neutron Jack, the former CEO of General Electric, who passed away in 2020, wasn't all business. Granted, there are some who will argue that, along with him, the 20th century idea of strong and heroic leadership should also disappear. Known for his candor and his competitive nature, he surely could not be described as "weak". In fact, one of his bestselling books was simply titled "Winning". However, don't be fooled. Even though he was demanding, decisive, and extremely competitive, Neutron Jack was known for exhibiting a great deal of vulnerability and a lot of emotion, for example in the letters he wrote to shareholders and employees. And that's what vulnerability is about. It's not about winning or losing, nor about being weak. It's about opening yourself up. And that's a serious business. So let's get to business.

We are conditioned to believe that emotions are less legitimate than thoughts, yet you can't think rationally if you are not emotional.

Can only the thick-skinned make it?

Emotions have derailed many careers. Crying on the job is a serious liability, and feelings have a bad reputation in business. However, that hasn't always been the case. According to Tom Lutz, upper-class men in the 18th century were supposed to cry on the job, otherwise they were seen as bullies. Yet, for one reason or another, we now prefer to see a more stoic attitude at work. And that's a real pity. Especially because confidence and compassion are not contradictory. In an interview, Jacinda Ardern, the prime minister of New Zealand, said: 'One of the criticisms I've faced over the years is that I'm not aggressive enough or assertive enough, or maybe somehow, because I'm empathetic, I'm weak. I totally rebel against that. I refuse to believe that you cannot be both compassionate and strong.'

Yet many studies have shown that people who show their emotions at work risk being perceived as less professional and less competent than their more stoic and "rational" colleagues. And countless emotional, empathic women and men have been advised to develop a thicker skin. The damage that has been done with this well-intended advice is considerable: it has given many leaders an excuse to stop listening to criticism and feedback, and to detach themselves from others' emotions and reactions altogether. Fortunately, in recent years, a strong antidote has been found: vulnerability.

Thanks to the world's vulnerability expert, Brené Brown, vulnerability has again become mainstream. Her books and TED Talks have created a movement consisting of professionals that embrace vulnerability and realize that this actually requires a lot of strength. In order to develop vulnerability we need to learn to accept our own emotions and those of others, instead of seeing them as dark forces that pull us away from our perfectly rational selves. By the way, if you do see emotions as a detraction, you might want to watch the kids' movie, "Inside Out". This movie illustrates perfectly how important emotions are to our overall functioning and well-being. Early on in the movie, the emotion of Joy controls the mind of the main character, Riley, a little girl who is always joyful and is rewarded by her environment for always being such a bundle of joy. Toward the end of the film, though, Joy—like Riley—learns that there is much more to being happy than constantly being cheerful and putting on a fake smile. In fact, in the film's final scene when Joy needs to hand over some of the control to her fellow emotions, such as Sadness, because Riley has difficulties adapting to a new home, Riley seems to achieve a deeper form of happiness. And that is precisely what emotions do: they help us to build deeper connections with others.

Of course, becoming more accepting of our own and others' emotions also requires us to sign up to get our asses kicked.

Heroes are scared too

Let's be real; people who stay in their comfort zone are not vulnerable at all. They can't make mistakes anymore. They can't fail. They're not risking anything. They also don't develop themselves. They don't learn. They don't grow beyond what they know. Do you really want to be that person?

In order to realize great things, you have to get out there. Into the non-comfort zone. And that feels scary. So don't mistakenly believe that the trailblazers of this world are nothing but confident and calm. In all likelihood, they feel their heart beating in their chest. Real courage is when you carry on even when you're nervous and unsure. You just need to flip the logic. It's not because you're scared that you are not brave. It is precisely the fact that you are scared that means that you are doing something brave. And when you feel all confident and cocky, are you really challenging yourself?

Wear your vulnerability like a badge of honor

Presenter Tom Bradby followed Meghan Markle, her husband Prince Harry, and their five-month-old son Archie throughout their African tour. The journey came after a whirlwind period in which the couple got engaged, got married (in the first interracial wedding in the English royal family), and Meghan got pregnant and had a baby, all under the immense scrutiny of the tabloids and even the serious press. When interviewing Meghan about all of that, Bradby asks her a very simple question: 'How are you?'. The very question seems to crack something in Meghan. She goes on to say: 'And, also thank you for asking, because not many people have asked if I'm OK. But it's a very real thing to be going through behind the scenes.' Bradby then goes on to ask Meghan if it is fair to say that it has been a struggle. Meghan replies: 'Yes', with her eyes going teary and seemingly trying to hold back more tears.

And, just like that, she was no longer a princess, but only a young mother struggling to keep it together. It's an interview that got worldwide attention, because it showed a person who is envied by the entire world showing the cracks in the façade of perfection, and revealing the vulnerable person behind it.

'We love seeing raw truth and openness in other people.'

We tend to think that showing vulnerability makes us look weak, inadequate, and flawed—a mess. But when others see our vulnerability, they might perceive something quite different, something alluring. 'We love seeing raw truth and openness in other people', Brené Brown writes in her book "Daring Greatly", 'but we're afraid to let them see it in us.'

Maybe it helps to bear in mind the "pratfall effect." Discovered in the 1960s, the pratfall effect shows that a little imperfection makes a person who is doing well overall seem more alluring than if they didn't have any imperfections at all. Do you remember the time that Jennifer Lawrence was awarded an Oscar? As she walked toward the stage in her full length ball gown, she tripped on the stairs, in front of the entire room and the millions watching at home. To stumble like that, precisely at the larger-than-life moment that crowned her career so far, was nothing but endearing. And that's exactly what the pratfall effect is about. Responses to someone's vulnerability do depend on how they are already perceived. It only works when you are already seen as competent. So, first give that killer presentation, and then spill your coffee. Not the other way around!

What we know for sure: you're a beautiful mess

Somehow, we are reluctant to exhibit vulnerability. Research by Bruk and her colleagues shows why this happens. She divided a group of students into two groups. The first group was asked to sing a song in front of a jury, which consisted of those in group two. Interestingly, the ones in the singing group held more negative opinions about vulnerability and found it to be repellent, while the jury members felt that vulnerability actually requires courage and strength. When we think about our own vulnerability, we focus on our imperfections. But when we think about others' vulnerability, it provides us with reassurances about the imperfections of others.

Bruk, A., S. G. Scholl, and H. Bless. (2018). Beautiful Mess Effect: Self-other Differences in Evaluation of Showing Vulnerability. *Journal of Personality and Social Psychology,* 115(2), 192-205.

We can all benefit from adopting a "beautiful mess" attitude and being okay with showing our vulnerability. When you are comfortable with your insecurities, it's easier for others to relate to you and open up to you. Take the group of CEOs who were dubbed the "cuddly CEOs" by the media when they confessed to falling into each other's arms when they meet at their regular retreats, during which they talk about their doubts and fears. But they oppose this term: 'Our message is too serious for that. Within the organization of the future, the CEO also constantly works on him or herself by focusing on introspection, adopting a vulnerable attitude, asking for feedback, and paying attention to personal growth.'

'I can't stop thinking about this - it has shaken me to the core,' Michelle Obama said. She was giving a speech on behalf of Hillary Clinton, to support her candidacy for president of the United States. But mostly she was talking about the derogatory comments about women that Donald Trump had made just a few days before. Her voice was trembling at times, the raw emotion palpable. It made the speech mesmerizing. You just couldn't stop listening to it, and it went viral the following days. What made it so different from any other political speech was the fact that Michelle Obama allowed her message to become so personal, and her emotion to be so visible. Whether that was sheer technique, or for real, it sure was mighty convincing. Good speakers use emotion to good effect. They know that showing it keeps the audience engaged. It's even been shown that, when a leader gives an inspiring speech filled with emotion, the audience is less likely to scrutinize the content of the message. But good speakers also know that you can't drive the emotion so far that you lose control. Oprah Winfrey would say: 'You can't go into the "ugly cry".'

Emotional intelligence is about being able to regulate and manage your emotions.

Emotional intelligence is about being able to regulate and manage your emotion so that you don't become a helpless victim of them. Paul Bulcke, chairman of Nestlé, explains how this works for him: 'Probably the most important thing I learned throughout my career is to practice detached involvement. It means you are fully aware of what's going on, you immerse yourself in whatever situation is going on, good or bad, but you're also able to detach yourself from it. There's always someone who will comment on your decisions. There's always going to be people who disagree. Everybody has an opinion. Especially with social media, it can make you feel naked. But you can't let that get to you too much or you'll lose all ability to make decisions or take action. You can't have your worry paralyze you. But you also should not develop thick skin. Because if you don't care anymore what anybody thinks or says, you become ignorant. You have to be aware, observe details, listen to people. But at the same time, you should be able to look at yourself as if you are in the audience, watching an actor on stage. Only in this case it's you being the actor in your own life. Detached involvement is about being an active participant and an observer of your life at the same time.'

What we know for sure: rock the boat but keep it steady

As a toddler, when you didn't like a situation you expressed it with a temper tantrum. Today, you have probably developed better techniques for making your discontent heard. But it's still emotion that is the driving force behind speaking up. Intense emotions, such as frustration, anger, and dissatisfaction, often drive people to challenge the status quo. Yet those very emotions can also be counterproductive. Because if you're overcome with emotion, you're just not very good at expressing your thoughts clearly and constructively. And your raw passion may be perceived as so in-your-face that the very people you want to convince back off. The trick is to be able to regulate your own emotions, and only then speak up.

People who are good at managing their emotions speak up more often. They're not afraid to voice their ideas and opinions, even if they rock the boat. And they're also not punished for challenging the status quo. On the contrary. They are seen as the high performers. But that's only true when they know how to regulate their emotions. Those who speak up frequently, and let their emotions run loose in doing so, risk only being seen as loose cannons.

As you may have learned as a 2-year-old: that temper tantrum only results in a time-out. By keeping your cool as you present your arguments, you may very well get exactly the change you want. (Note by Marion: as my 12-year-old has clearly discovered in negotiating screen time with a well-prepared PowerPoint.)

Grant, A. (2013). Rocking the Boat but Keeping it Steady: The Role of Emotion Regulation in Employee Voice. *Academy of Management Journal,* 56(6), 1703-1723.

In essence, it all boils down to not suppressing our emotions altogether, but, at the same time, not being a slave to our emotions either. We need to start treating our emotions like data—and we all know what happens when we ignore the data. Many people don't treat their emotions as data, but develop more dysfunctional emotional patterns. Susan David found out that some of these dysfunctional patterns involve bottling and brooding. Bottling is the habit of ignoring the data and pushing your difficult emotions aside by rationalizing them. You literally put a lid on your emotions. But we know what happens if you shake a bottle of soda and you then take the lid off ... you will get it back in your face. Brooding, on the other hand, reflects a tendency to dwell on negative emotions, and to go over your emotions repeatedly, which may result in you over-analyzing those negative emotions. This can lead to great distress and anxiety. The way to deal with bottling and brooding is to recognize your own pattern and recognize when you are hooked by your emotions. Are you a bottler or a brooder? A second step is to label your emotions. When our emotions get the better of us, we often don't have the mental space to examine them. One proven strategy that helps you to deal with a situation is accepting that there is an emotion by labelling it. The third step is to not suppress the emotion, but to accept it and allow yourself to experience the emotion. Finally, when you have managed your emotion, rather than controlled it, you can decide to act in a way that aligns with your personal values. So, in fact, it's all about treating your own and others' emotions as external data, rather than being hooked by them.

Take it from us

Vulnerability has always intrigued us—and we admit that we have also struggled with it.

Somehow we seem to appreciate vulnerability in others, but when we are the ones in a vulnerable position, we feel naked. Yet vulnerability makes us human, and that can be very reassuring for others. After all, who wants to work with a stoic Mister or Miss Perfect? That's just intimidating! And who wants to be led by a robotic machine? Absolutely nobody. So we have come to learn that you can be both strong and vulnerable at the same time. And you shouldn't even hide it.

When you take the leap, do it with confidence.

14 Be your own boss

The myth: freelancers and entrepreneurs have easy, flexible lives

I want to break free.

Freddie Mercury

'Free at last! Free at last! Thank God almighty we are free at last!' These are the words of Martin Luther King Jr. But they might as well be the words of the newborn independent worker who has relieved him or herself from the shackles of corporate life. Are you also dreaming of doing your "own thing"? Your own thing involving being your own boss, and working from wherever you want, whenever you want. Making your own decisions and setting your own schedule, but also, first and foremost, making your own dreams come alive. After all, whose childhood dream was it to work nine-to-five to make a living? We're pretty sure that your land of make-believe as a child did not look anything like 'tumbling out of bed, stumbling to the kitchen, and pouring yourself a cup of ambition' in order to head to a dull office, where life was filled with long meetings, endless commutes, draining phone calls, and constantly juggling and balancing agendas. And, if you are completely honest with yourself, perhaps you still find yourself daydreaming of dropping out of pay-check-style altogether. And perhaps that's exactly what you'd do if you had no constraints in life, no expectations from friends and family, and no financial limitations holding you back from taking the leap? So, do you feel ready to strike out on your own?

Work as a series of gigs

Oh, the freelancer's freedom! Staying in your pajamas doing computer work until mid-afternoon. Finally giving in to the fact that you'll never be a morning person, and changing the 9-to-5 to a 12- to-8. The freedom to say no to a job you just don't feel like doing. Just because you can.

If that sounds like the ideal life to you, it seems that you may not be the only one. On a global level, the number of "gig workers", i.e. workers who perform small, individual projects on an independent, autonomous, and flexible (freelance) basis, is on the rise. Currently, the number of gig workers is estimated to be 20% of the active working population and some studies predict that, due to digitization, this number will increase to around 40% in the next decade ... which means that there is an almost 1 in 2 chance that, by then, you will be a "gig worker" too. Perhaps you may even be combining multiple gigs simultaneously! Clearly, the future of work is not what it used to be. And that future seems to be here already!

From the outside, the freelancer's life can seem pretty attractive. But the research is also pretty clear.

From the outside, the freelancer's life can seem pretty attractive. But the research is also pretty clear. Freelance work has many benefits, but it will not solve all of the problems that you are trying to escape from when you are working in a traditional job. Gig work is not the holy grail of work that you may be dreaming of. Because it also involves doing your own administration, working overtime, chasing for clients, and making sure your bills are paid. This is surely not part of your dreams, right? Let's face it, even though companies can be dehumanizing places, with all of their policies, job descriptions, and procedures to hold you back, they also provide a safe environment, where you are not only relatively sure of getting your paychecks but where you can also build strong social connections and find meaning by contributing to something that is bigger than yourself.

The hard reality is that gig workers experience not only social isolation but also great uncertainty about their income, future opportunities, and quality of life. All of that, while also being confronted with the same constraints as traditional workers. Does that mean that, as a gig worker, you're doomed to lead a life of disappointment and uncertainty? Of course not. Far from it. What it does mean is that it is important to be realistic. As a gig worker, you may be in a permanent love/hate relationship with your life choice. So, before you take the leap, you may also want to consider some alternatives. Because what we also know for sure is that a new world of work is emerging inside traditional organizations, as many companies are radically rethinking their entire approach to work design. Self-managed teams, tribes and squads, and project work are all the rage in the model organization. Therefore, even working for the same organization can offer you the chance to jump from "gig" to "gig".

You may also want to consider some alternatives as a new world of work is emerging inside traditional organizations.

Martine Polen, a freelance coach, recalls: 'In 2012, I quit my safe and fun desk job to become a freelancer. Some of my friends and family members thought I was crazy. But I felt that there was more to life than doing a 9-to-5 office job with fixed responsibilities. I wanted more variety in content and context, and to pursue my passions ... basically I wanted to do my own thing, whatever that meant. And so, I started a master's in executive coaching and became a freelance coach. Even though I do not regret my choice at all, I also recognize that I had some naïve conceptions of freelance work. I thought I could hang out in my comfy clothes all day, decide on my own schedule. And that I could work with the people of my choice, in the places I want, whenever that suited me. While there is truth in some of this, surprise, surprise, the reality is a little bit different. Also, while I indeed have a network of great clients who I love to work for, the work is not always exhilarating, some clients prefer to use freelancers to do their "dirty" work. And while working remotely from a great destination, being available for the children, or learning new skills when it suits me sounds like a real perk of freelance work, more often than not, I am on the exact same schedule as my clients. That said, freelance work has made me courageous. I have worked on assignments that could never have happened if I had not been a freelancer. So despite all the hard work, and the resistance I encountered, it has been an amazing experience. I have crafted my own path and that path had its ups and downs ... and despite the downs, the path does feel like "my own thing".'

What does it take to succeed as a gig worker? Funnily enough, it may be that you need to create your own version of corporate life. Michael Bond, the inventor of Paddington Bear, once confessed: 'I have been writing every day of my life, seven days a week, for almost 50 years. Even Christmas Day. But I still enjoy it. I have lived in the same house for the last 30 years and I have written in the same room ever since. I am at my desk every morning at 9 a.m.'

What we know for sure: how to live the dream by staying connected

So, what does the research say? Is it possible to do your own thing and overcome the uncertainty that gig work brings with it? Recent studies have mapped out the skills that gig workers need in order to function well in their new environment. How can you stay resilient and ensure that you do not become demoralized and completely isolated? In order to really thrive as a gig worker, it is important that you build four types of connections: location, routine, people, and goal.

1/ Connection with location

Many of us think that one of the biggest advantages of the gig economy is that you can work where and when you want. Research shows that those who function best in the gig economy are often those who choose to work in a (limited) number of places, and at relatively fixed times. So, even if the work permits full flexibility, the most successful gig workers choose to avoid as many distractions as possible by creating a fixed workplace and working at fixed times. It enables them to maintain a better balance between work and their personal life.

2/ Incorporating routines

The most successful gig workers also appear to create a number of fixed routines. It may sound counterintuitive, but it is quite consistent with previous research into atypical professions, which has shown that the most successful writers, artists, and even elite athletes stick to a relatively fixed routine. Routine offers structure, which means that you waste less energy on organizing yourself. For the most successful gig workers, the devil was in the detail. Some started the day by reading the newspaper for 15 minutes, others had a bath, and others chose a daily afternoon nap at 12.15 p.m. In other words, they created a certain rigidity within the flexibility of the job. The energy they saved could be used for other things, such as creativity and developing new skills.

3/ Connections with people

The most successful gig workers also continue investing in their networks. They are highly aware of the risk of social isolation and they actively take steps to avoid that, even if they are not naturally inclined to want social interaction. Of the three types of networks we looked at in chapter 9, the most successful gig workers invest most in their development network. That is the network you turn to for advice, or for a listening ear when you feel insecure. By investing in such a network, the most successful gig workers get the encouragement and recognition they need to function well.

4/ Connection with a goal

And finally, perhaps a somewhat esoteric connection that the most successful gig workers appear to strive for is the connection with their goal. Their personal life goal you could say. That connection with their goal ensures that they do not respond to every opportunity that comes their way, but they mainly grab and create opportunities that will enable them to reach their higher goal. In other words, by having a goal for themselves, the most successful gig workers ensure that routine does not become a silent killer. The goal also functions as an internal compass so they know which "gigs" suit them.

By building these four important connections in their daily working life, successful gig workers develop their own definition of success. It is a definition that is not always objectifiable according to traditional standards, but it subjectively gives them the feeling of really living. Perhaps we can all learn from this.

Petriglieri, G., S. Ashford, and A. Wrzesniewski. (2018). Agony and Ecstasy in the Gig Economy: Cultivating Holding Environments for Precarious and Personalized Work Identities. *Administrative Science Quarterly*, 64 (1), 124-170.

Employing yourself ... and others

Maybe your dreams go further than just employing yourself. You want to be an entrepreneur, starting a real business. The first step may feel like a giant leap. 'The hardest thing about starting a business is actually starting it', says Louis Jonckheere, co-founder of Showpad.

About 10% of people want to start up their own business at some time in the near future.

About 10% of people want to start up their own business at some time in the near future. A lot less do it in reality. This is because they're afraid of failing and don't really have faith in their own capabilities. There's a gigantic gap between dreams and reality. Many entrepreneurs only really go for it when they have no other options left. Just as creativity is born out of necessity, entrepreneurship is often born out of a lack of alternatives. It's hard to leave the golden cage as long as it's there to protect you. But the longer you postpone your dream, the more distant it may appear. When Jeff Bezos started with Amazon, he had a high-flying job on Wall Street as the senior vice president of a hedge fund. Starting to sell books from his garage must not have seemed like a career progression. But he took the leap anyway: 'I had to project myself forward to age 80. I don't want to be 80 years old, cataloguing a bunch of major regrets of my life.'

That sentiment of not wanting any regrets is echoed in the story of Mette Lykke, co-founder of Endomondo. 'Becoming an entrepreneur just felt right. At the time, I was working for McKinsey. And even though we talked a lot about impact, I longed to solve a real issue. And I wanted more flexibility in my life. When we had a birthday party in the family, I wanted to be the one deciding that I could go there, and not be stuck with a work assignment. Being able to make the calls myself was part of my motivation. But mostly, I thought, if this is the dream I have, I should just really do it. What is the total cost over a lifetime? What's the worst that can happen? If you fail and 2-3 years later you need to go back to your previous job, that's not the end of the world. Becoming an entrepreneur gives you an education you cannot get anywhere. At worst, you have just learned a lot. The risk in making that jump is more your pride and ego. You don't want to be a failure.'

Yes, the risk of failure is an integral part of being an entrepreneurial innovator. It was certainly part of the story of Endomondo. Founded in 2007 in Copenhagen, it was one of the first applications to track and share your workouts. But it came to the market early, and the context was not exactly favorable. As Mette remembers: 'My co-founders and myself were resigning simultaneously from McKinsey to focus on Endomondo. And a lot of people told us we were crazy. This was just before the financial crisis, so we launched at a time when the economic climate was difficult. The idea we had was also ahead of its time. An app based on GPS technology, even before the iPhone existed. Only a couple of phones had GPS connectivity. It took a long time to get traction. We needed to wait for the adoption of smartphones. It was super hard to find investors, we got money wherever we could find it. There were 50 no's for every yes. And every time we needed to find another angle. And every time a door closed we looked for a window to get in. It was just always like that, being resourceful and not taking no for an answer. That has been a great learning curve.'

Overnight success and exponential growth are much rarer than you may think. But rocky roads can also lead to wonderful destinations.

Overnight success and exponential growth are much rarer than you may think. But rocky roads can also lead to wonderful destinations. While Endomondo came to the market early, all of the players that ended up defining that workout tracking space were founded around that time. Today, Endomondo is part of Under Armour, and counts 30 million users. Mette Lykke moved on and is now CEO of social impact company Too Good To Go.

The entrepreneurial path is one where you take control of your own destiny and build something yourself. But that does not mean it's the path of ultimate freedom. Even if you don't have an employer to nag you, you will have the people who give you financial backing, your customers, etc. And you will feel an enormous sense of responsibility toward the people you employ or the people that support you financially. As Mette Lykke recalls: 'Suddenly you have people who put all their money in you. That's an insane pressure to have! Even if it was high pressure at McKinsey, it was nothing compared to that. So sometimes I'm concerned that we promote entrepreneurship too much, because it is not for everybody. It takes stamina. I have seen young people who would be better off in a job with a manager and somebody that makes their workload manageable.'

The entrepreneurial path is one where you take control of your own destiny and build something yourself. But that does not mean it's the path of ultimate freedom.

Take it from us

We all need to bear the consequences of our decisions ... and also of our career decisions. When you decide to pursue a freelance career, you may need to learn that with much flexibility also comes much responsibility. When you venture out as an entrepreneur, you may figure out that nobody is fully their own boss. And when you decide to stay within the safer boundaries of an organization, you also need to accept the constraints that may come with that. But, in the end, you can never rise beyond the limitations of your beliefs. If you believe that you can't thrive and be resilient as a freelancer, you won't be able to thrive and be resilient. If you believe that you can't start a successful business, you will never run a successful business. So when you take the leap, do it with confidence. And let's not forget: at the end of the day, whatever career path you choose, you can never escape accountability. We might be able to escape the accountability toward a boss, but at the end of the day there is always someone holding us accountable: shareholders, clients, family ... and, most importantly, ourselves.

What difference do you want to make?

15 Create your own ripple effect

The myth: one person cannot change the world

Just as ripples spread out when a single pebble is dropped into water, the actions of individuals can have far-reaching effects.

Dalai Lama

By a twisted turn of events, we are writing this final chapter in the midst of the COVID-19 pandemic, each of us sitting in our sunny home offices (ok, we admit: thanks to good weather karma we are on our outside patios), with slightly too much caffeine intake. We are both experiencing this new normal in our own way. One of us is living through this situation as the dean of Vlerick, with the obvious leadership challenges that come with undertaking such a role in an unprecedented context (note from Katleen: and she's doing it with glory). The other is living the reality that she's been teaching about: leading in turbulence. Despite our different roles, there are also many similarities that unite us. We empathize with the uncertainty faced by the entrepreneurs we work with. We worry about the health of colleagues, participants and loved ones. And, all of a sudden, we feel some anxiety when going to the supermarket (we never would have thought that shopping could have such an effect on us). And we both have our kids sitting next to us, doing their homework, while we are writing this closing chapter. A humbling experience—the type of experience that forces you to reflect on yourself as a leader and on what you bring to this situation. A moment to pause and think about the difference you want to make. Not only for your colleagues and customers, but also for those kids sitting next to you. It's all too easy to look at a situation like this and see it as something that you can't possibly influence. But if there is one lesson that this situation has taught us, it is that there is a lot of truth in the old cliché: every individual makes a difference. And we don't mean this in a shallow way. The ruthless reality is that every single person has a vital responsibility resting on his/her shoulders. Just because you carry the title of "dean" or "professor" that doesn't mean that washing your hands will have a greater impact on the national health situation. No matter who "you" are, if you don't stay at home then you're basically jeopardizing others' health. And the role of individual responsibility applies to many situations. If you put your money in a secret account in Panama, while telling yourself a story that it is technically perfectly legal to do so, then someone else will ultimately pay the price for that. It is as simple as that. And that's the message we want to convey in this closing chapter. No matter what your formal role is, no matter how big or small you think you are, every single individual's choices and behaviors impact the greater good in significant ways. So how will you contribute? What difference do you want to make?

The ruthless reality is that every single person has a vital responsibility resting on his/her shoulders.

Optimism is a moral duty

Every single day we're bombarded with reports about how the world is going to hell. We hear stories about war, sickness, poverty, abuse, pollution, and so on. Such messages can pull even the greatest optimist into a pit of despair. But Karl Popper and Immanuel Kant were right. Optimism is a moral duty. It's a duty for those of us who have the privilege of being able to read a book and reflect on our work lives. If we can't show optimism, then who can? Being an optimist doesn't mean that you should walk around with perennially rose-colored glasses, oblivious to the threats and problems in the world. That would be irresponsible. But so is being pessimistic. As Winston Churchill said, 'For myself I am an optimist - it does not seem to be much use to be anything else'. Despite the headlines, the world is getting better. So let's take Bill and Melinda Gates, who are outspoken about their optimism, as examples. The newsletter of the Bill & Melinda Gates Foundation is even pointedly titled "The Optimist". In spite of this, it's clear that the goals that Bill and Melinda have set for themselves are elusive. Even with the help of fellow gazillionaire friends, such as Warren Buffett. (Buffett, who just like Bill Gates is one of the top 5 richest people on this planet, famously vowed to donate the bulk of his fortune to his friend's foundation.) The Bill & Melinda Gates foundation aims to tackle global problems, such as infectious diseases, child mortality, and inclusive economic growth. But even though Bill Gates predicted in 2015 the type of pandemic we are now suffering through with COVID-19, he could not prevent it. And even though Melinda vowed to spend $1 billion to fight gender inequality, she admits that is not nearly enough: '$1 billion is a lot of money, but I also recognize that it's only a small fraction of what's necessary'. It is now 20 years since Bill and Melinda began work on their foundation and their work isn't nearly done. But that does not make them any less optimistic: 'Being an optimist isn't about knowing that life used to be worse. It's about knowing how life can get better. And that's what really should fuel our optimism'. An optimist sees the world in perspective, expresses gratitude for the progress that has been made, and knows that the road ahead is the one to an even better place.

The primary ingredient for progress is optimism.

Because, in the end, Simon Sinek is right: 'The primary ingredient for progress is optimism'. Because if you don't believe that things can be better, you'll never be driven to action. It's the fundamental belief that it is possible to positively impact the world that inspires creativity and progress. Yet, when we think about progress, we often think of achieving big goals or major breakthroughs. And that's not what's necessary. Realistic optimists get their energy from small wins and are in it for the long haul. Because, indeed, relentless pursuit is what is needed.

Your ripple effect

So should you first start a company, grow it to be the biggest software firm in the world, amass a fortune in doing so, then use that fortune to solve the world's issues and only then have a real impact? Sounds like a plan? Don't despair. We don't need to be Bill Gates in order to have an impact on the world.

Of course, none of us can change the entire world all by ourselves—and if you believe that you can, then you might suffer from the dark triad we described in chapter 10. But you can be the change that you want to see. By making small adjustments to our own lives and by encouraging others to do the same, we can create a ripple effect that can eventually impact our entire planet. Sounds a bit too idealistic for you? Then think again ...

'We can't just continue living as if there was no tomorrow, because there is a tomorrow. That's all we are saying.' It's a simple and somewhat inconvenient truth, delivered by a teenage girl with Asperger syndrome that none of us had ever heard of until August 2018. A girl that started spending her school days outside the Swedish parliament to call for stronger action on climate change. That girl was Greta Thunberg. Of course, not everybody mobilizes the world at the age of sweet sixteen. But if there is one thing we can learn from Greta Thunberg, it's that it is never too early to start thinking about what you want to leave behind.

We are not telling you to live your life like a saint. We aren't saints either, far from it. So make your mistakes and learn from them. But realize that the path to losing your integrity is a gradual one. Consider the story of John Dean, White House counsel to President Nixon. In his biography, "Blind Ambition", Dean describes how he rapidly ascended through the ranks of government ... and the story ends with his conviction and imprisonment for his role in the Watergate cover-up. It would be easy to read John Dean's memoirs and judge him as being a "bad person". But, let's face it, Dean was just an inexperienced leader who quickly rose to a very powerful position, for which he was ill prepared.

The path of least resistance

In today's dynamic and turbulent environment, leaders who do not have a strong moral compass are likely to struggle to live up to their own values. But it would be wrong to assume that we start our careers with a completely developed moral compass. We all need to learn how to make ethical judgment calls. Following the path of least resistance can be tempting. Taking credit for the hard work of a colleague, remaining a bystander when questionable practices are undertaken, using your role to engage in self-serving behavior ... there are many situations that could entice you to follow the less ethical route. And you might even have rational reasons for committing such minor (or not so minor) transgressions. After all, didn't you also have to work in the shadows to get to where you are today? And if no one else tells the emperor that (s)he's naked, why should you? But you know what: two wrongs don't make a right. Research into the psychology of immoral behavior by Vikas Anand and Blake Ashforth shows that even the smallest of "sins" can escalate into worse types of unethical and immoral behavior if they are repeated and rationalized. Rationalizations are by far the biggest enemies of integrity. Rationalizations work like tranquilizers. They paralyze us and help us to avoid the pain of guilt. But don't be mistaken. Just like the song by Red Zebra predicts: tranquilizers will ultimately make you nervous.

Of course, what is considered to be good is often controversial. Just as the path to losing your integrity is a gradual one, so is the path to keeping it intact. It's not a matter of "having" or "not having" integrity. Being ethical isn't a binary thing. The only thing you can strive for is to become more ethical as you progress on your life journey. But what we know for sure is that doing good is about more than avoiding doing anything wrong. As Yvon Chouinard, the founder of the sustainable outdoor clothing corporation Patagonia, said: 'If you're not part of the solution, then you're part of the problem'. So the choice is simple: are you part of the solution or part of the problem? There is no middle way.

Being part of the solution doesn't necessarily mean that your solutions to complex problems always need to be comprehensive and all-encompassing. In fact, in the bestselling book "The Tipping Point", Malcolm Gladwell highlights that Band-Aid solutions are often more likely to change society for the better than very comprehensive ones. Band-Aids are simple, convenient and very flexible solutions to an amazing amount of problems, ranging from fixing shoes and tennis rackets to cell phones. Many of us feel reluctant to impact society because we feel it won't make a difference and because we feel that a Band-Aid can't fix the problems in the world. But sometimes the simplest solutions have the biggest impact, because of the ripple effects they create. An inspiring example of a simple solution is the Akshar School, a small school that started in the Himalayas in India. As a way to make school more accessible and help clean up their local community, this primary school began to accept grocery bags full of plastic waste instead of school fees. If you google "Akshar School", you'll see pictures of children lining up in front of the school, arms filled with plastic bottles and packaging.

Sometimes the simplest solutions have the biggest impact, because of the ripple effects they create.

Doing better is good, doing good is even better

When giving a commencement speech to graduating students, Oprah Winfrey told them to ask themselves one very simple question: 'What will your essential service be?'

As an individual, you can make a positive social impact through many facets of life—from your choice of career, to what you purchase. It might be as simple as changing your consumer behavior, contributing to charity, or starting up your own business with positive social impact at the core. One of the most important things to remember about social impact is that, as an individual, you do make a difference. Even though the problems of the world may seem overwhelming, by doing your bit you can make a huge difference. Social impact is about making choices that support the greater good, and in order to make the biggest social impact we all need to feel empowered and feel that we can make a difference.

Françoise Chombar, CEO of the microelectronic systems' company Melexis, shared the following advice to our MBA students: 'Many of you are pursuing this MBA because you want to do better. And doing better is good. But you know what? Doing good is even better.' Yvon Chouinard, the founder of Patagonia, expresses a similar sentiment. He has been in business for almost sixty years, but he still feels uncomfortable with calling himself a businessman: 'It's as difficult for me to say those words, as it is for someone to admit being an alcoholic or a lawyer. It's business that has to take the majority of the blame for being the enemy of nature, for destroying native cultures, from taking from the poor and giving to the rich. Yet business can produce food, cure disease, control population, employ people, and generally enrich our lives. And it can do these good things and make a profit without losing its soul.'

Close to home

Thinking about your ripple effect can be daunting. We can't all be tackling the world's problems! And when you are still carving your own path, it's incredibly difficult to think about the impact you could have beyond yourself and to act on it. Most days, you're just getting by, trying to conquer the day instead of conquering the world. Who has time to think about their legacy? Isn't that something for people close to retirement or wealthy do-gooders?

But, really, you don't have to search very far for it. Some of the world's most successful people realize that their ripple effect can be found very close to home. In fact, it's staring you right in the face. Because your most important impact is the day-to-day impact that you have on the people around you. In the words of Oprah Winfrey: 'The best piece of advice I ever received came from my friend and writer Maya Angelou. Your legacy is all of the lives you touched. It's what you do every day.' Paul Bulcke agrees: 'Don't think of your legacy as something grand. Think of it as the mark you made on people that matter to you.'

So, ultimately it comes down to the contours of the shadow you throw on the people around you. Are you kind? Are you honest? Are you gracious and grateful? Are you paying forward what you received from others? That's doing good.

Take it from us

Throughout this book, we have often focused on your role in the pursuit of your own personal happiness. At the end, we dare you to consider the idea that your personal happiness is dependent on the impact you have on others. Ask yourself what your ripple effect will be. But we, the authors of this book, also have our role to play. That's why we are donating the proceeds of this book to the Vlerick Spirit Scholarship Fund, to help talented young people unlock their full potential. As business educators, it is our aim and commitment to develop leaders and entrepreneurs who have a positive impact on society. A quick look at the business news section of any newspaper teaches us that there is more to be done. But that's another story, for another time.

Sources of inspiration

Our main source of inspiration comes from the multitude of people we are lucky enough to meet through our professional activities. They include the business leaders we engage with and coach in the Vlerick executive programs, and the many MBA and Masters students we educate. We hope we inspired them, but the truth is that they inspire us at least as much.

We are also ferocious and somewhat eclectic readers and listeners. The academic sources to the research projects we discuss in our "What we know for sure" pieces are included throughout the book.

Next to these, here's a list of things that inspire us:

Podcasts:

- Armchair Expert with Dax Shepard
- HBR Ideacast
- After Hours
- Ear Biscuits
- Marathon Training Academy
- Next Question with Katie Couric
- Unlocking Us with Brené Brown
- Revisionist History with Malcolm Gladwell
- Sampler
- States of Mind
- The Happiness Lab
- TED Talks Daily

- Why should anyone be led by you? What it takes to be an authentic leader with Rob Goffee and Gareth Jones
- ZIGO [in Dutch]

Books we read and enjoyed recently and some golden oldies too:

- 21 Letters on Life and its Challenges, Charles Handy
- 21 Lessons for the 21st Century, Yuval Noah Harari
- Act Like a Leader, Think Like a Leader, Herminia Ibarra
- Edge, Laura Huang
- Emotional Agility, Susan David
- Durf!, Bart Verhaeghe [in Dutch]
- Dare to Lead, Brené Brown
- Give and Take, Adam Grant
- Good Night Stories for Rebel Girls, Elena Favilli Francesca Cavallo
- Le Petit Prince, Antoine de Saint-Exupéry
- Man's Search for Meaning, Victor Frankl
- Mindset, Carol Dweck
- Oh, the Places You'll Go, Dr. Seuss
- Pippi Longstocking, Astrid Lindgren
- Stories for Boys who Dare to be Different, Ben Brooks
- The Algebra of Happiness, Scott Galloway
- To the Desert and Back, Philip Mirvis, Karen Ayas, and George Roth
- Trailblazer, Marc Benioff
- True North: Discover Your Authentic Leadership, Bill George & Peter Sims
- Tipping Point, Malcolm Gladwell

- There Are No Grown-Ups, Pamela Druckerman
- Becoming, Michelle Obama
- Option B, Sheryl Sandberg & Adam Grant
- What I Talk About When I Talk About Running, Haruki Murakami
- What I Know for Sure, Oprah Winfrey